CHINESE NAMES, SURNAMES, LOCATIONS & ADDRESSES

中国大陆地址集

BEIJING MUNICIPALITY - PART 1

北京直辖市

ZIYUE TANG

汤子玥

ACKNOWLEDGEMENT

I am deeply indebted to my friends and family members to support me throughout my life. Without their invaluable love and guidance, this work wouldn't have been possible.

Thank you

Ziyue Tang

汤子玥

PREFACE

The book introduces foreigner students to the Chinese names along with locations and addresses from the **Beijing** Municipality of China (中国北京直辖市). The book contains 150 entries (names, addresses) explained with simplified Chinese characters, pinyin and English.

Chinese names follow the standard convention where the given name is written after the surname. For example, in 王威 (Wang Wei), Wang is the surname, and Wei is the given name. Further, the surnames are generally made of one (王) or two characters (司马). Similarly, the given names are also made of either one or two characters. For example, 司马威 (Sima Wei) is a three character Chinese name suitable for men. 司马威威 is a four character Chinese name.

Chinese addresses are comprised of different administrative units that start with the largest geographic entity (country) and continue to the smallest entity (county, building names, room number). For example, a typical address in Nanjing city (capital of Jiangsu province) would look like 江苏省南京市清华路 28 栋 520 室 (Jiāngsū shěng nánjīng shì qīnghuá lù 28 dòng 520 shì; Room 520, Building 28, Qinghua Road, Nanjing City, Jiangsu Province).

CONTENTS

CHAPTER 1: NAME, SURNAME & ADDRESSES (1-30)

1。姓名: 相寰顺

住址（公司）：中国北京市昌平区智钢路 945 号国圣有限公司（邮政编码：111643）。联系电话：14327384。电子邮箱：daiue@egvmlcao.biz.cn

Zhù zhǐ: Xiàng Huán Shùn Zhōng Guó Běijīng Shì Chāngpíng Qū Zhì Gāng Lù 945 Hào Guó Shèng Yǒuxiàn Gōngsī (Yóuzhèng Biānmǎ：111643). Liánxì Diànhuà：14327384. Diànzǐ Yóuxiāng：daiue@egvmlcao.biz.cn

Huan Shun Xiang, Guo Sheng Corporation, 945 Zhi Gang Road, Changping District, Beijing, China. Postal Code: 111643. Phone Number：14327384. E-mail：daiue@egvmlcao.biz.cn

2。姓名: 洪鹤翰

住址（博物院）：中国北京市石景山区禹辙路 113 号北京博物馆（邮政编码：987471）。联系电话：69332822。电子邮箱：oasvh@xbjpseog.museums.cn

Zhù zhǐ: Hóng Hè Hàn Zhōng Guó Běijīng Shì Shíjǐngshān Qū Yǔ Zhé Lù 113 Hào Běijīng Bó Wù Guǎn (Yóuzhèng Biānmǎ：987471). Liánxì Diànhuà：69332822. Diànzǐ Yóuxiāng：oasvh@xbjpseog.museums.cn

He Han Hong, Beijing Museum, 113 Yu Zhe Road, Shijingshan District, Beijing, China. Postal Code: 987471. Phone Number：69332822. E-mail：oasvh@xbjpseog.museums.cn

3。姓名: 郑龙己

住址（机场）：中国北京市密云区民勇路 913 号北京舟舟国际机场（邮政编码：111523）。联系电话：27863156。电子邮箱：iwhkd@gueapyvc.airports.cn

Zhù zhǐ: Zhèng Lóng Jǐ Zhōng Guó Běijīng Shì Mìyún Qū Mín Yǒng Lù 913 Hào Běijīng Zhōu Zhōu Guó Jì Jī Chǎng (Yóuzhèng Biānmǎ：111523). Liánxì Diànhuà：27863156. Diànzǐ Yóuxiāng：iwhkd@gueapyvc.airports.cn

Long Ji Zheng, Beijing Zhou Zhou International Airport, 913 Min Yong Road, Miyun District, Beijing, China. Postal Code: 111523. Phone Number：27863156. E-mail：iwhkd@gueapyvc.airports.cn

4。姓名: 盛熔科

住址（博物院）：中国北京市石景山区腾庆路 929 号北京博物馆（邮政编码：673631）。联系电话：76119355。电子邮箱：fpdgt@nuysxwlf.museums.cn

Zhù zhǐ: Shèng Róng Kē Zhōng Guó Běijīng Shì Shíjǐngshān Qū Téng Qìng Lù 929 Hào Běijīng Bó Wù Guǎn (Yóuzhèng Biānmǎ：673631). Liánxì Diànhuà：76119355. Diànzǐ Yóuxiāng：fpdgt@nuysxwlf.museums.cn

Rong Ke Sheng, Beijing Museum, 929 Teng Qing Road, Shijingshan District, Beijing, China. Postal Code: 673631. Phone Number：76119355. E-mail：fpdgt@nuysxwlf.museums.cn

5。姓名: 亓官铁不

住址（寺庙）：中国北京市怀柔区翼可路 539 号轶山寺（邮政编码：191023）。联系电话：71460219。电子邮箱：wlcgp@adfyujhi.god.cn

Zhù zhǐ: Qíguān Fū Bù Zhōng Guó Běijīng Shì Huáiróu Qū Yì Kě Lù 539 Hào Yì Shān Sì (Yóuzhèng Biānmǎ：191023). Liánxì Diànhuà：71460219. Diànzǐ Yóuxiāng：wlcgp@adfyujhi.god.cn

Fu Bu Qiguan, Yi Shan Temple, 539 Yi Ke Road, Huairou District, Beijing, China. Postal Code: 191023. Phone Number：71460219. E-mail：wlcgp@adfyujhi.god.cn

6。姓名: 牧冕南

住址（家庭）：中国北京市房山区晖波路 296 号跃炯公寓 44 层 149 室（邮政编码：289885）。联系电话：24828501。电子邮箱：lxhyi@siecaort.cn

Zhù zhǐ: Mù Miǎn Nán Zhōng Guó Běijīng Shì Fáng Shān Qū Huī Bō Lù 296 Hào Yuè Jiǒng Gōng Yù 44 Céng 149 Shì (Yóuzhèng Biānmǎ：289885). Liánxì Diànhuà：24828501. Diànzǐ Yóuxiāng：lxhyi@siecaort.cn

Mian Nan Mu, Room# 149, Floor# 44, Yue Jiong Apartment, 296 Hui Bo Road, Fangshan District, Beijing, China. Postal Code: 289885. Phone Number：24828501. E-mail：lxhyi@siecaort.cn

7。姓名: 百里食昌

住址（机场）：中国北京市密云区友隆路 636 号北京稼淹国际机场（邮政编码：493287）。联系电话：11609525。电子邮箱：evhfr@pwtmruyi.airports.cn

Zhù zhǐ: Bǎilǐ Shí Chāng Zhōng Guó Běijīng Shì Mìyún Qū Yǒu Lóng Lù 636 Hào Běijīng Jià Yān Guó Jì Jī Chǎng (Yóuzhèng Biānmǎ：493287). Liánxì Diànhuà：11609525. Diànzǐ Yóuxiāng：evhfr@pwtmruyi.airports.cn

Shi Chang Baili, Beijing Jia Yan International Airport, 636 You Long Road, Miyun District, Beijing, China. Postal Code: 493287. Phone Number：11609525. E-mail：evhfr@pwtmruyi.airports.cn

8。姓名: 贾炯白

住址（医院）：中国北京市密云区振胜路 232 号尚昌医院（邮政编码：851383）。联系电话：77847553。电子邮箱：tusyv@hrjwumfp.health.cn

Zhù zhǐ: Jiǎ Jiǒng Bái Zhōng Guó Běijīng Shì Mìyún Qū Zhèn Shēng Lù 232 Hào Shàng Chāng Yī Yuàn (Yóuzhèng Biānmǎ：851383). Liánxì Diànhuà：77847553. Diànzǐ Yóuxiāng：tusyv@hrjwumfp.health.cn

Jiong Bai Jia, Shang Chang Hospital, 232 Zhen Sheng Road, Miyun District, Beijing, China. Postal Code: 851383. Phone Number：77847553. E-mail：tusyv@hrjwumfp.health.cn

9。姓名: 喻大咚

住址（大学）：中国北京市丰台区浩跃大学学居路 630 号（邮政编码：209854）。联系电话：67462275。电子邮箱：deyxb@ymjazpvw.edu.cn

Zhù zhǐ: Yù Dài Dōng Zhōng Guó Běijīng Shì Fēngtái Qū Hào Yuè DàxuéXué Jū Lù 630 Hào（Yóuzhèng Biānmǎ：209854). Liánxì Diànhuà：67462275. Diànzǐ Yóuxiāng：deyxb@ymjazpvw.edu.cn

Dai Dong Yu, Hao Yue University, 630 Xue Ju Road, Fengtai District, Beijing, China. Postal Code: 209854. Phone Number：67462275. E-mail：deyxb@ymjazpvw.edu.cn

10。姓名: 东门冠智

住址（寺庙）：中国北京市密云区翰尚路 593 号波其寺（邮政编码：780432）。联系电话：17213265。电子邮箱：nvqdf@tyvdxrlb.god.cn

Zhù zhǐ: Dōngmén Guān Zhì Zhōng Guó Běijīng Shì Mìyún Qū Hàn Shàng Lù 593 Hào Bō Qí Sì（Yóuzhèng Biānmǎ：780432). Liánxì Diànhuà：17213265. Diànzǐ Yóuxiāng：nvqdf@tyvdxrlb.god.cn

Guan Zhi Dongmen, Bo Qi Temple, 593 Han Shang Road, Miyun District, Beijing, China. Postal Code: 780432. Phone Number：17213265. E-mail：nvqdf@tyvdxrlb.god.cn

11。姓名: 隗成化

住址（酒店）：中国北京市石景山区超亭路 790 号郁豹酒店（邮政编码：845584）。联系电话：19101641。电子邮箱：ecaqw@goyisjcb.biz.cn

Zhù zhǐ: Kuí Chéng Huā Zhōng Guó Běijīng Shì Shíjǐngshān Qū Chāo Tíng Lù 790 Hào Yù Bào Jiǔ Diàn (Yóuzhèng Biānmǎ：845584). Liánxì Diànhuà：19101641. Diànzǐ Yóuxiāng：ecaqw@goyisjcb.biz.cn

Cheng Hua Kui, Yu Bao Hotel, 790 Chao Ting Road, Shijingshan District, Beijing, China. Postal Code: 845584. Phone Number：19101641. E-mail：ecaqw@goyisjcb.biz.cn

12。姓名: 通化嘉

住址（寺庙）：中国北京市延庆区钦大路 249 号桥庆寺（邮政编码：322115）。联系电话：55536538。电子邮箱：xbeai@codretjx.god.cn

Zhù zhǐ: Tōng Huà Jiā Zhōng Guó Běijīng Shì Yánqìng Qū Qīn Dà Lù 249 Hào Qiáo Qìng Sì (Yóuzhèng Biānmǎ：322115). Liánxì Diànhuà：55536538. Diànzǐ Yóuxiāng：xbeai@codretjx.god.cn

Hua Jia Tong, Qiao Qing Temple, 249 Qin Da Road, Yanqing District, Beijing, China. Postal Code: 322115. Phone Number：55536538. E-mail：xbeai@codretjx.god.cn

13。姓名: 酆食臻

住址（公司）：中国北京市丰台区鹤屹路 573 号歧山有限公司（邮政编码：238951）。联系电话：18371151。电子邮箱：nqewi@ypqsjtdo.biz.cn

Zhù zhǐ: Fēng Shí Zhēn Zhōng Guó Běijīng Shì Fēngtái Qū Hè Yì Lù 573 Hào Qí Shān Yǒuxiàn Gōngsī (Yóuzhèng Biānmǎ：238951). Liánxì Diànhuà：18371151. Diànzǐ Yóuxiāng：nqewi@ypqsjtdo.biz.cn

Shi Zhen Feng, Qi Shan Corporation, 573 He Yi Road, Fengtai District, Beijing, China. Postal Code: 238951. Phone Number：18371151. E-mail：nqewi@ypqsjtdo.biz.cn

14。姓名: 於斌威

住址（机场）：中国北京市东城区近中路 253 号北京葛计国际机场（邮政编码：451177）。联系电话：65440753。电子邮箱：
xztbe@qwceaibv.airports.cn

Zhù zhǐ: Yū Bīn Wēi Zhōng Guó Běijīng Shì Dōng Chéng Qū Jìn Zhōng Lù 253 Hào Běijīng Gé Jì Guó Jì Jī Chǎng (Yóuzhèng Biānmǎ：451177). Liánxì Diànhuà：65440753. Diànzǐ Yóuxiāng：xztbe@qwceaibv.airports.cn

Bin Wei Yu, Beijing Ge Ji International Airport, 253 Jin Zhong Road, Dongcheng Area, Beijing, China. Postal Code: 451177. Phone Number：65440753. E-mail：
xztbe@qwceaibv.airports.cn

15。姓名: 阙来臻

住址（寺庙）：中国北京市密云区圣秀路 782 号易宽寺（邮政编码：238237）。联系电话：84060867。电子邮箱：fbkjl@lapdhune.god.cn

Zhù zhǐ: Quē Lái Zhēn Zhōng Guó Běijīng Shì Mìyún Qū Shèng Xiù Lù 782 Hào Yì Kuān Sì (Yóuzhèng Biānmǎ：238237). Liánxì Diànhuà：84060867. Diànzǐ Yóuxiāng：fbkjl@lapdhune.god.cn

Lai Zhen Que, Yi Kuan Temple, 782 Sheng Xiu Road, Miyun District, Beijing, China. Postal Code: 238237. Phone Number：84060867. E-mail：
fbkjl@lapdhune.god.cn

16。姓名: 夏侯冠甫

住址（湖泊）：中国北京市延庆区队敬路 751 号炯楚湖（邮政编码：897762）。联系电话：26052850。电子邮箱：yszco@sxpdehbi.lakes.cn

Zhù zhǐ: Xiàhóu Guàn Fǔ Zhōng Guó Běijīng Shì Yánqìng Qū Duì Jìng Lù 751 Hào Jiǒng Chǔ Hú (Yóuzhèng Biānmǎ：897762). Liánxì Diànhuà：26052850. Diànzǐ Yóuxiāng：yszco@sxpdehbi.lakes.cn

Guan Fu Xiahou, Jiong Chu Lake, 751 Dui Jing Road, Yanqing District, Beijing, China. Postal Code: 897762. Phone Number：26052850. E-mail：yszco@sxpdehbi.lakes.cn

17。姓名: 钦其学

住址（大学）：中国北京市平谷区维汉大学土兆路 129 号（邮政编码：480465）。联系电话：72223809。电子邮箱：egqjt@pomfhldg.edu.cn

Zhù zhǐ: Qīn Qí Xué Zhōng Guó Běijīng Shì Pínggǔ Qū Wéi Hàn DàxuéTǔ Zhào Lù 129 Hào（Yóuzhèng Biānmǎ：480465). Liánxì Diànhuà：72223809. Diànzǐ Yóuxiāng：egqjt@pomfhldg.edu.cn

Qi Xue Qin, Wei Han University, 129 Tu Zhao Road, Pinggu District, Beijing, China. Postal Code: 480465. Phone Number：72223809. E-mail：egqjt@pomfhldg.edu.cn

18。姓名: 苏迅人

住址（家庭）：中国北京市平谷区其强路 487 号食惟公寓 50 层 954 室（邮政编码：652854）。联系电话：17429254。电子邮箱：ksvqg@tnlaimrg.cn

Zhù zhǐ: Sū Xùn Rén Zhōng Guó Běijīng Shì Pínggǔ Qū Qí Qiáng Lù 487 Hào Yì Wéi Gōng Yù 50 Céng 954 Shì (Yóuzhèng Biānmǎ：652854). Liánxì Diànhuà：17429254. Diànzǐ Yóuxiāng：ksvqg@tnlaimrg.cn

Xun Ren Su, Room# 954, Floor# 50, Yi Wei Apartment, 487 Qi Qiang Road, Pinggu District, Beijing, China. Postal Code: 652854. Phone Number：17429254. E-mail：ksvqg@tnlaimrg.cn

19。姓名: 夹谷亚沛

住址（湖泊）：中国北京市海淀区红钦路 860 号仓勇湖（邮政编码：601768）。联系电话：27504407。电子邮箱：entli@ifpojcrn.lakes.cn

Zhù zhǐ: Jiágǔ Yà Bèi Zhōng Guó Běijīng Shì Hǎidiàn Qū Hóng Qīn Lù 860 Hào Cāng Yǒng Hú（Yóuzhèng Biānmǎ：601768）. Liánxì Diànhuà：27504407. Diànzǐ Yóuxiāng：entli@ifpojcrn.lakes.cn

Ya Bei Jiagu, Cang Yong Lake, 860 Hong Qin Road, Haidian District, Beijing, China. Postal Code: 601768. Phone Number：27504407. E-mail：entli@ifpojcrn.lakes.cn

20。姓名: 贡坡世

住址（公共汽车站）：中国北京市昌平区咚渊路 646 号冠际站（邮政编码：721111）。联系电话：77760309。电子邮箱：drfyl@abrmnhwf.transport.cn

Zhù zhǐ: Gòng Pō Shì Zhōng Guó Běijīng Shì Chāngpíng Qū Dōng Yuān Lù 646 Hào Guàn Jì Zhàn（Yóuzhèng Biānmǎ：721111). Liánxì Diànhuà：77760309. Diànzǐ Yóuxiāng：drfyl@abrmnhwf.transport.cn

Po Shi Gong, Guan Ji Bus Station, 646 Dong Yuan Road, Changping District, Beijing, China. Postal Code: 721111. Phone Number：77760309. E-mail：drfyl@abrmnhwf.transport.cn

21。姓名: 索澜游

住址（公园）：中国北京市昌平区强跃路 635 号发铭公园（邮政编码：246653）。联系电话：66570860。电子邮箱：nzbct@pvaghxuf.parks.cn

Zhù zhǐ: Suǒ Lán Yóu Zhōng Guó Běijīng Shì Chāngpíng Qū Qiǎng Yuè Lù 635 Hào Fā Míng Gōng Yuán（Yóuzhèng Biānmǎ：246653). Liánxì Diànhuà：66570860. Diànzǐ Yóuxiāng：nzbct@pvaghxuf.parks.cn

Lan You Suo, Fa Ming Park, 635 Qiang Yue Road, Changping District, Beijing, China. Postal Code: 246653. Phone Number：66570860. E-mail：nzbct@pvaghxuf.parks.cn

22。姓名: 舒亮腾

住址（博物院）：中国北京市朝阳区敬臻路 557 号北京博物馆（邮政编码：982065）。联系电话：85792875。电子邮箱：ulqwt@gloyprdm.museums.cn

Zhù zhǐ: Shū Liàng Téng Zhōng Guó Běijīng Shì Zhāoyáng Qū Jìng Zhēn Lù 557 Hào Běijīng Bó Wù Guǎn（Yóuzhèng Biānmǎ：982065）. Liánxì Diànhuà：85792875. Diànzǐ Yóuxiāng：ulqwt@gloyprdm.museums.cn

Liang Teng Shu, Beijing Museum, 557 Jing Zhen Road, Chaoyang District, Beijing, China. Postal Code: 982065. Phone Number：85792875. E-mail：ulqwt@gloyprdm.museums.cn

23。姓名: 霍守勇

住址（家庭）：中国北京市大兴区乙盛路 241 号原智公寓 17 层 365 室（邮政编码：526445）。联系电话：49972734。电子邮箱：iquna@ugdjiwsl.cn

Zhù zhǐ: Huò Shǒu Yǒng Zhōng Guó Běijīng Shì Dàxīng Qū Yǐ Chéng Lù 241 Hào Yuán Zhì Gōng Yù 17 Céng 365 Shì (Yóuzhèng Biānmǎ：526445). Liánxì Diànhuà：49972734. Diànzǐ Yóuxiāng：iquna@ugdjiwsl.cn

Shou Yong Huo, Room# 365, Floor# 17, Yuan Zhi Apartment, 241 Yi Cheng Road, Daxing District, Beijing, China. Postal Code: 526445. Phone Number：49972734. E-mail：iquna@ugdjiwsl.cn

24。姓名: 聂强民

住址（广场）：中国北京市朝阳区宝磊路 905 号轶隆广场（邮政编码：365227）。联系电话：72068166。电子邮箱：yhvzn@bnezsgkp.squares.cn

Zhù zhǐ: Niè Qiáng Mín Zhōng Guó Běijīng Shì Zhāoyáng Qū Bǎo Lěi Lù 905 Hào Yì Lóng Guǎng Chǎng（Yóuzhèng Biānmǎ：365227）. Liánxì Diànhuà：72068166. Diànzǐ Yóuxiāng：yhvzn@bnezsgkp.squares.cn

Qiang Min Nie, Yi Long Square, 905 Bao Lei Road, Chaoyang District, Beijing, China. Postal Code: 365227. Phone Number：72068166. E-mail：yhvzn@bnezsgkp.squares.cn

25。姓名: 谯冠威

住址（广场）：中国北京市房山区帆尚路 830 号珏智广场（邮政编码：117537）。联系电话：65761670。电子邮箱：dqkwa@nlkexjzh.squares.cn

Zhù zhǐ: Qiáo Guàn Wēi Zhōng Guó Běijīng Shì Fáng Shān Qū Fān Shàng Lù 830 Hào Jué Zhì Guǎng Chǎng（Yóuzhèng Biānmǎ：117537). Liánxì Diànhuà：65761670. Diànzǐ Yóuxiāng：dqkwa@nlkexjzh.squares.cn

Guan Wei Qiao, Jue Zhi Square, 830 Fan Shang Road, Fangshan District, Beijing, China. Postal Code: 117537. Phone Number：65761670. E-mail：dqkwa@nlkexjzh.squares.cn

26。姓名: 项石龙

住址（机场）：中国北京市昌平区星石路 472 号北京自彬国际机场（邮政编码：880918）。联系电话：48045351。电子邮箱：asibz@woshykzj.airports.cn

Zhù zhǐ: Xiàng Dàn Lóng Zhōng Guó Běijīng Shì Chāngpíng Qū Xīng Shí Lù 472 Hào Běijīng Zì Bīn Guó Jì Jī Chǎng（Yóuzhèng Biānmǎ：880918). Liánxì Diànhuà：48045351. Diànzǐ Yóuxiāng：asibz@woshykzj.airports.cn

Dan Long Xiang, Beijing Zi Bin International Airport, 472 Xing Shi Road, Changping District, Beijing, China. Postal Code: 880918. Phone Number：48045351. E-mail：asibz@woshykzj.airports.cn

27。姓名: 廖盛敬

住址（广场）：中国北京市顺义区仓盛路 817 号维石广场（邮政编码：345433）。联系电话：68142200。电子邮箱：ytopu@jrgcxpts.squares.cn

Zhù zhǐ: Liào Shèng Jìng Zhōng Guó Běijīng Shì Shùnyì Qū Cāng Shèng Lù 817 Hào Wéi Dàn Guǎng Chǎng（Yóuzhèng Biānmǎ：345433). Liánxì Diànhuà：68142200. Diànzǐ Yóuxiāng：ytopu@jrgcxpts.squares.cn

Sheng Jing Liao, Wei Dan Square, 817 Cang Sheng Road, Shunyi District, Beijing, China. Postal Code: 345433. Phone Number：68142200. E-mail：ytopu@jrgcxpts.squares.cn

28。姓名: 向食队

住址（广场）：中国北京市通州区民全路 374 号继翼广场（邮政编码：569893）。联系电话：70384902。电子邮箱：bfyis@ubtsylic.squares.cn

Zhù zhǐ: Xiàng Yì Duì Zhōng Guó Běijīng Shì Tōngzhōu Qū Mín Quán Lù 374 Hào Jì Yì Guǎng Chǎng（Yóuzhèng Biānmǎ：569893). Liánxì Diànhuà：70384902. Diànzǐ Yóuxiāng：bfyis@ubtsylic.squares.cn

Yi Dui Xiang, Ji Yi Square, 374 Min Quan Road, Tongzhou District, Beijing, China. Postal Code: 569893. Phone Number：70384902. E-mail：bfyis@ubtsylic.squares.cn

29。姓名: 西门大寰

住址（火车站）：中国北京市怀柔区领征路 254 号北京站（邮政编码：798631）。联系电话：85203140。电子邮箱：sphto@cirvnezx.chr.cn

Zhù zhǐ: Xīmén Dài Huán Zhōng Guó Běijīng Shì Huáiróu Qū Lǐng Zhēng Lù 254 Hào Běijīng Zhàn（Yóuzhèng Biānmǎ：798631). Liánxì Diànhuà：85203140. Diànzǐ Yóuxiāng：sphto@cirvnezx.chr.cn

Dai Huan Ximen, Beijing Railway Station, 254 Ling Zheng Road, Huairou District, Beijing, China. Postal Code: 798631. Phone Number：85203140. E-mail：sphto@cirvnezx.chr.cn

30。姓名: 佴彬亮

住址（大学）：中国北京市昌平区铭食大学乙豪路 142 号（邮政编码：954596）。联系电话：99730385。电子邮箱：ifvpc@zqepuwda.edu.cn

Zhù zhǐ: Nài Bīn Liàng Zhōng Guó Běijīng Shì Chāngpíng Qū Míng Sì DàxuéYǐ Háo Lù 142 Hào (Yóuzhèng Biānmǎ：954596). Liánxì Diànhuà：99730385. Diànzǐ Yóuxiāng：ifvpc@zqepuwda.edu.cn

Bin Liang Nai, Ming Si University, 142 Yi Hao Road, Changping District, Beijing, China. Postal Code: 954596. Phone Number：99730385. E-mail：ifvpc@zqepuwda.edu.cn

CHAPTER 2: NAME, SURNAME & ADDRESSES (31-60)

31。姓名: 纪愈兵

住址（广场）：中国北京市密云区金强路 442 号豹仓广场（邮政编码：235680）。联系电话：18065535。电子邮箱：pkebn@ovptexmd.squares.cn

Zhù zhǐ: Jì Yù Bīng Zhōng Guó Běijīng Shì Mìyún Qū Jīn Qiáng Lù 442 Hào Bào Cāng Guǎng Chǎng（Yóuzhèng Biānmǎ：235680). Liánxì Diànhuà：18065535. Diànzǐ Yóuxiāng：pkebn@ovptexmd.squares.cn

Yu Bing Ji, Bao Cang Square, 442 Jin Qiang Road, Miyun District, Beijing, China. Postal Code: 235680. Phone Number：18065535. E-mail：pkebn@ovptexmd.squares.cn

32。姓名: 祖渊来

住址（大学）：中国北京市房山区昌熔大学淘勇路 678 号（邮政编码：986082）。联系电话：79564878。电子邮箱：xmoue@wqdlejus.edu.cn

Zhù zhǐ: Zǔ Yuān Lái Zhōng Guó Běijīng Shì Fáng Shān Qū Chāng Róng DàxuéXún Yǒng Lù 678 Hào（Yóuzhèng Biānmǎ：986082). Liánxì Diànhuà：79564878. Diànzǐ Yóuxiāng：xmoue@wqdlejus.edu.cn

Yuan Lai Zu, Chang Rong University, 678 Xun Yong Road, Fangshan District, Beijing, China. Postal Code: 986082. Phone Number：79564878. E-mail：xmoue@wqdlejus.edu.cn

33。姓名: 牧迅迅

住址（医院）：中国北京市延庆区己继路 213 号石稼医院（邮政编码：538079）。联系电话：93749346。电子邮箱：ymbnd@vyapjzel.health.cn

Zhù zhǐ: Mù Xùn Xùn Zhōng Guó Běijīng Shì Yánqìng Qū Jǐ Jì Lù 213 Hào Shí Jià Yī Yuàn（Yóuzhèng Biānmǎ：538079). Liánxì Diànhuà：93749346. Diànzǐ Yóuxiāng：ymbnd@vyapjzel.health.cn

Xun Xun Mu, Shi Jia Hospital, 213 Ji Ji Road, Yanqing District, Beijing, China. Postal Code: 538079. Phone Number：93749346. E-mail：ymbnd@vyapjzel.health.cn

34。姓名: 阳葛鸣

住址（寺庙）：中国北京市门头沟区陆胜路 400 号舟珏寺（邮政编码：644328）。联系电话：35029273。电子邮箱：evciu@bfxelamy.god.cn

Zhù zhǐ: Yáng Gé Míng Zhōng Guó Běijīng Shì Méntóugōu Qū Lù Shēng Lù 400 Hào Zhōu Jué Sì (Yóuzhèng Biānmǎ：644328). Liánxì Diànhuà：35029273. Diànzǐ Yóuxiāng：evciu@bfxelamy.god.cn

Ge Ming Yang, Zhou Jue Temple, 400 Lu Sheng Road, Mentougou District, Beijing, China. Postal Code: 644328. Phone Number：35029273. E-mail：evciu@bfxelamy.god.cn

35。姓名: 禄焯黎

住址（机场）：中国北京市房山区陶毅路 783 号北京屹游国际机场（邮政编码：785499）。联系电话：61714222。电子邮箱：agroy@fnhymjpv.airports.cn

Zhù zhǐ: Lù Chāo Lí Zhōng Guó Běijīng Shì Fáng Shān Qū Táo Yì Lù 783 Hào Běijīng Yì Yóu Guó Jì Jī Chǎng (Yóuzhèng Biānmǎ：785499). Liánxì Diànhuà：61714222. Diànzǐ Yóuxiāng：agroy@fnhymjpv.airports.cn

Chao Li Lu, Beijing Yi You International Airport, 783 Tao Yi Road, Fangshan District, Beijing, China. Postal Code: 785499. Phone Number：61714222. E-mail：agroy@fnhymjpv.airports.cn

36。姓名: 陶嘉禹

住址（机场）：中国北京市海淀区国愈路 821 号北京祥不国际机场（邮政编码：218687）。联系电话：32868954。电子邮箱：losqc@cgswhuvq.airports.cn

Zhù zhǐ: Táo Jiā Yǔ Zhōng Guó Běijīng Shì Hǎidiàn Qū Guó Yù Lù 821 Hào Běijīng Xiáng Bù Guó Jì Jī Chǎng (Yóuzhèng Biānmǎ：218687). Liánxì Diànhuà：32868954. Diànzǐ Yóuxiāng：losqc@cgswhuvq.airports.cn

Jia Yu Tao, Beijing Xiang Bu International Airport, 821 Guo Yu Road, Haidian District, Beijing, China. Postal Code: 218687. Phone Number：32868954. E-mail：losqc@cgswhuvq.airports.cn

37。姓名: 司空自晖

住址（大学）：中国北京市怀柔区辉化大学岐迅路 841 号（邮政编码：931078）。联系电话：15777993。电子邮箱：rfanx@kpmqlwhj.edu.cn

Zhù zhǐ: Sīkōng Zì Huī Zhōng Guó Běijīng Shì Huáiróu Qū Huī Huā DàxuéQí Xùn Lù 841 Hào (Yóuzhèng Biānmǎ：931078). Liánxì Diànhuà：15777993. Diànzǐ Yóuxiāng：rfanx@kpmqlwhj.edu.cn

Zi Hui Sikong, Hui Hua University, 841 Qi Xun Road, Huairou District, Beijing, China. Postal Code: 931078. Phone Number：15777993. E-mail：rfanx@kpmqlwhj.edu.cn

38。姓名: 辛钢成

住址（寺庙）：中国北京市海淀区化自路 288 号刚辉寺（邮政编码：828269）。联系电话：44407337。电子邮箱：srubd@rlygefvk.god.cn

Zhù zhǐ: Xīn Gāng Chéng Zhōng Guó Běijīng Shì Hǎidiàn Qū Huà Zì Lù 288 Hào Gāng Huī Sì (Yóuzhèng Biānmǎ：828269). Liánxì Diànhuà：44407337. Diànzǐ Yóuxiāng：srubd@rlygefvk.god.cn

Gang Cheng Xin, Gang Hui Temple, 288 Hua Zi Road, Haidian District, Beijing, China. Postal Code: 828269. Phone Number：44407337. E-mail：srubd@rlygefvk.god.cn

39。姓名: 满焯胜

住址（大学）：中国北京市东城区坤威大学陆宽路 170 号（邮政编码：626978）。联系电话：58220492。电子邮箱：dwijq@auyhxrts.edu.cn

Zhù zhǐ: Mǎn Zhuō Shēng Zhōng Guó Běijīng Shì Dōng Chéng Qū Kūn Wēi DàxuéLiù Kuān Lù 170 Hào （Yóuzhèng Biānmǎ：626978). Liánxì Diànhuà：58220492. Diànzǐ Yóuxiāng：dwijq@auyhxrts.edu.cn

Zhuo Sheng Man, Kun Wei University, 170 Liu Kuan Road, Dongcheng Area, Beijing, China. Postal Code: 626978. Phone Number：58220492. E-mail：dwijq@auyhxrts.edu.cn

40。姓名: 芮豪队

住址（广场）：中国北京市通州区锤大路 149 号译白广场（邮政编码：905020）。联系电话：34963087。电子邮箱：vcpfn@uavyqzgh.squares.cn

Zhù zhǐ: Ruì Háo Duì Zhōng Guó Běijīng Shì Tōngzhōu Qū Chuí Dài Lù 149 Hào Yì Bái Guǎng Chǎng （Yóuzhèng Biānmǎ：905020). Liánxì Diànhuà：34963087. Diànzǐ Yóuxiāng：vcpfn@uavyqzgh.squares.cn

Hao Dui Rui, Yi Bai Square, 149 Chui Dai Road, Tongzhou District, Beijing, China. Postal Code: 905020. Phone Number：34963087. E-mail：vcpfn@uavyqzgh.squares.cn

41。姓名: 秋桥昌

住址（酒店）：中国北京市西城区兆轶路 911 号食绅酒店（邮政编码：663384）。联系电话：63256273。电子邮箱：wujpo@jmskwxep.biz.cn

Zhù zhǐ: Qiū Qiáo Chāng Zhōng Guó Běijīng Shì Xī Chéng Qū Zhào Yì Lù 911 Hào Sì Shēn Jiǔ Diàn （Yóuzhèng Biānmǎ：663384). Liánxì Diànhuà：63256273. Diànzǐ Yóuxiāng：wujpo@jmskwxep.biz.cn

Qiao Chang Qiu, Si Shen Hotel, 911 Zhao Yi Road, Xicheng District, Beijing, China. Postal Code: 663384. Phone Number：63256273. E-mail：wujpo@jmskwxep.biz.cn

42。姓名：司楚来

住址（寺庙）：中国北京市海淀区隆谢路 574 号晗翼寺（邮政编码：469031）。联系电话：39270780。电子邮箱：lkjvf@bfxhctwi.god.cn

Zhù zhǐ: Sī Chǔ Lái Zhōng Guó Běijīng Shì Hǎidiàn Qū Lóng Xiè Lù 574 Hào Hán Yì Sì (Yóuzhèng Biānmǎ：469031). Liánxì Diànhuà：39270780. Diànzǐ Yóuxiāng：lkjvf@bfxhctwi.god.cn

Chu Lai Si, Han Yi Temple, 574 Long Xie Road, Haidian District, Beijing, China. Postal Code: 469031. Phone Number：39270780. E-mail：lkjvf@bfxhctwi.god.cn

43。姓名：桂仲员

住址（火车站）：中国北京市昌平区坚超路 593 号北京站（邮政编码：806509）。联系电话：25358933。电子邮箱：basnd@gurwclpy.chr.cn

Zhù zhǐ: Guì Zhòng Yuán Zhōng Guó Běijīng Shì Chāngpíng Qū Jiān Chāo Lù 593 Hào Běijīng Zhàn (Yóuzhèng Biānmǎ：806509). Liánxì Diànhuà：25358933. Diànzǐ Yóuxiāng：basnd@gurwclpy.chr.cn

Zhong Yuan Gui, Beijing Railway Station, 593 Jian Chao Road, Changping District, Beijing, China. Postal Code: 806509. Phone Number：25358933. E-mail：basnd@gurwclpy.chr.cn

44。姓名：吕德源

住址（机场）：中国北京市门头沟区振原路 314 号北京绅波国际机场（邮政编码：501280）。联系电话：31232742。电子邮箱：pwizg@qsvyumxe.airports.cn

Zhù zhǐ: Lǚ Dé Yuán Zhōng Guó Běijīng Shì Méntóugōu Qū Zhèn Yuán Lù 314 Hào Běijīng Shēn Bō Guó Jì Jī Chǎng (Yóuzhèng Biānmǎ：501280). Liánxì Diànhuà：31232742. Diànzǐ Yóuxiāng：pwizg@qsvyumxe.airports.cn

De Yuan Llv, Beijing Shen Bo International Airport, 314 Zhen Yuan Road, Mentougou District, Beijing, China. Postal Code: 501280. Phone Number：31232742. E-mail：pwizg@qsvyumxe.airports.cn

45。姓名: 堵翰员

住址（家庭）：中国北京市门头沟区淹星路 462 号惟寰公寓 23 层 287 室（邮政编码：661510）。联系电话：22449571。电子邮箱：vidsz@vgzqojke.cn

Zhù zhǐ: Dǔ Hàn Yuán Zhōng Guó Běijīng Shì Méntóugōu Qū Yān Xīng Lù 462 Hào Wéi Huán Gōng Yù 23 Céng 287 Shì (Yóuzhèng Biānmǎ：661510). Liánxì Diànhuà：22449571. Diànzǐ Yóuxiāng：vidsz@vgzqojke.cn

Han Yuan Du, Room# 287, Floor# 23, Wei Huan Apartment, 462 Yan Xing Road, Mentougou District, Beijing, China. Postal Code: 661510. Phone Number：22449571. E-mail：vidsz@vgzqojke.cn

46。姓名: 陆乐奎

住址（广场）：中国北京市平谷区祥炯路 757 号圣星广场（邮政编码：556840）。联系电话：19944939。电子邮箱：pwmjh@czrkahsq.squares.cn

Zhù zhǐ: Lù Lè Kuí Zhōng Guó Běijīng Shì Pínggǔ Qū Xiáng Jiǒng Lù 757 Hào Shèng Xīng Guǎng Chǎng（Yóuzhèng Biānmǎ：556840). Liánxì Diànhuà：19944939. Diànzǐ Yóuxiāng：pwmjh@czrkahsq.squares.cn

Le Kui Lu, Sheng Xing Square, 757 Xiang Jiong Road, Pinggu District, Beijing, China. Postal Code: 556840. Phone Number：19944939. E-mail：pwmjh@czrkahsq.squares.cn

47。姓名: 容陆泽

住址（机场）：中国北京市朝阳区盛勇路 204 号北京盛鸣国际机场（邮政编码：285737）。联系电话：53649329。电子邮箱：avhcb@uoylfwpq.airports.cn

Zhù zhǐ: Róng Liù Zé Zhōng Guó Běijīng Shì Zhāoyáng Qū Chéng Yǒng Lù 204 Hào Běijīng Shèng Míng Guó Jì Jī Chǎng（Yóuzhèng Biānmǎ：285737）. Liánxì Diànhuà：53649329. Diànzǐ Yóuxiāng：avhcb@uoylfwpq.airports.cn

Liu Ze Rong, Beijing Sheng Ming International Airport, 204 Cheng Yong Road, Chaoyang District, Beijing, China. Postal Code: 285737. Phone Number：53649329. E-mail：avhcb@uoylfwpq.airports.cn

48。姓名: 孔磊兆

住址（公司）：中国北京市石景山区黎智路 174 号翰石有限公司（邮政编码：570985）。联系电话：50022304。电子邮箱：dyhtq@drfkwjqb.biz.cn

Zhù zhǐ: Kǒng Lěi Zhào Zhōng Guó Běijīng Shì Shíjǐngshān Qū Lí Zhì Lù 174 Hào Hàn Shí Yǒuxiàn Gōngsī（Yóuzhèng Biānmǎ：570985). Liánxì Diànhuà：50022304. Diànzǐ Yóuxiāng：dyhtq@drfkwjqb.biz.cn

Lei Zhao Kong, Han Shi Corporation, 174 Li Zhi Road, Shijingshan District, Beijing, China. Postal Code: 570985. Phone Number：50022304. E-mail：dyhtq@drfkwjqb.biz.cn

49。姓名: 丁仓臻

住址（公司）：中国北京市通州区仲冠路 912 号骥奎有限公司（邮政编码：744212）。联系电话：83867204。电子邮箱：ktlhf@yntezluf.biz.cn

Zhù zhǐ: Dīng Cāng Zhēn Zhōng Guó Běijīng Shì Tōngzhōu Qū Zhòng Guān Lù 912 Hào Jì Kuí Yǒuxiàn Gōngsī（Yóuzhèng Biānmǎ：744212). Liánxì Diànhuà：83867204. Diànzǐ Yóuxiāng：ktlhf@yntezluf.biz.cn

Cang Zhen Ding, Ji Kui Corporation, 912 Zhong Guan Road, Tongzhou District, Beijing, China. Postal Code: 744212. Phone Number：83867204. E-mail：ktlhf@yntezluf.biz.cn

50。姓名: 郎伦晖

住址（广场）：中国北京市石景山区继金路 656 号铭发广场（邮政编码：929459）。联系电话：93074895。电子邮箱：mdkwq@tmifeohu.squares.cn

Zhù zhǐ: Láng Lún Huī Zhōng Guó Běijīng Shì Shíjǐngshān Qū Jì Jīn Lù 656 Hào Míng Fā Guǎng Chǎng（Yóuzhèng Biānmǎ：929459). Liánxì Diànhuà：93074895. Diànzǐ Yóuxiāng：mdkwq@tmifeohu.squares.cn

Lun Hui Lang, Ming Fa Square, 656 Ji Jin Road, Shijingshan District, Beijing, China. Postal Code: 929459. Phone Number：93074895. E-mail：mdkwq@tmifeohu.squares.cn

51。姓名: 诸葛冕自

住址（酒店）：中国北京市通州区彬化路 621 号民顺酒店（邮政编码：983922）。联系电话：30149272。电子邮箱：xgaum@limstxuw.biz.cn

Zhù zhǐ: Zhūgě Miǎn Zì Zhōng Guó Běijīng Shì Tōngzhōu Qū Bīn Huà Lù 621 Hào Mín Shùn Jiǔ Diàn（Yóuzhèng Biānmǎ：983922). Liánxì Diànhuà：30149272. Diànzǐ Yóuxiāng：xgaum@limstxuw.biz.cn

Mian Zi Zhuge, Min Shun Hotel, 621 Bin Hua Road, Tongzhou District, Beijing, China. Postal Code: 983922. Phone Number：30149272. E-mail：xgaum@limstxuw.biz.cn

52。姓名: 习自汉

住址（公园）：中国北京市丰台区茂译路 889 号原自公园（邮政编码：706211）。联系电话：91922040。电子邮箱：repcg@zasbqdjv.parks.cn

Zhù zhǐ: Xí Zì Hàn Zhōng Guó Běijīng Shì Fēngtái Qū Mào Yì Lù 889 Hào Yuán Zì Gōng Yuán（Yóuzhèng Biānmǎ：706211). Liánxì Diànhuà：91922040. Diànzǐ Yóuxiāng：repcg@zasbqdjv.parks.cn

Zi Han Xi, Yuan Zi Park, 889 Mao Yi Road, Fengtai District, Beijing, China. Postal Code: 706211. Phone Number：91922040. E-mail：repcg@zasbqdjv.parks.cn

53。姓名: 侯钊勇

住址（湖泊）：中国北京市延庆区易南路 379 号人铭湖（邮政编码：803016）。联系电话：61475623。电子邮箱：hlrpy@sxuywihq.lakes.cn

Zhù zhǐ: Hóu Zhāo Yǒng Zhōng Guó Běijīng Shì Yánqìng Qū Yì Nán Lù 379 Hào Rén Míng Hú（Yóuzhèng Biānmǎ：803016). Liánxì Diànhuà：61475623. Diànzǐ Yóuxiāng：hlrpy@sxuywihq.lakes.cn

Zhao Yong Hou, Ren Ming Lake, 379 Yi Nan Road, Yanqing District, Beijing, China. Postal Code: 803016. Phone Number：61475623. E-mail：hlrpy@sxuywihq.lakes.cn

54。姓名: 余王国

住址（公共汽车站）：中国北京市通州区龙焯路 855 号锤际站（邮政编码：615219）。联系电话：23548657。电子邮箱：ovkjq@dzyfgnps.transport.cn

Zhù zhǐ: Yú Wáng Guó Zhōng Guó Běijīng Shì Tōngzhōu Qū Lóng Chāo Lù 855 Hào Chuí Jì Zhàn（Yóuzhèng Biānmǎ：615219). Liánxì Diànhuà：23548657. Diànzǐ Yóuxiāng：ovkjq@dzyfgnps.transport.cn

Wang Guo Yu, Chui Ji Bus Station, 855 Long Chao Road, Tongzhou District, Beijing, China. Postal Code: 615219. Phone Number：23548657. E-mail：ovkjq@dzyfgnps.transport.cn

55。姓名: 司马珂石

住址（公共汽车站）：中国北京市大兴区咚屹路 718 号淹乐站（邮政编码：264100）。联系电话：19005358。电子邮箱：nqhgb@puedhgav.transport.cn

Zhù zhǐ: Sīmǎ Kē Dàn Zhōng Guó Běijīng Shì Dàxīng Qū Dōng Yì Lù 718 Hào Yān Lè Zhàn（Yóuzhèng Biānmǎ：264100). Liánxì Diànhuà：19005358. Diànzǐ Yóuxiāng：nqhgb@puedhgav.transport.cn

Ke Dan Sima, Yan Le Bus Station, 718 Dong Yi Road, Daxing District, Beijing, China. Postal Code: 264100. Phone Number：19005358. E-mail：nqhgb@puedhgav.transport.cn

56。姓名: 阚葆全

住址（公司）：中国北京市密云区圣智路 730 号晖沛有限公司（邮政编码：656850）。联系电话：55588723。电子邮箱：icomw@syazfvhd.biz.cn

Zhù zhǐ: Kàn Bǎo Quán Zhōng Guó Běijīng Shì Mìyún Qū Shèng Zhì Lù 730 Hào Huī Pèi Yǒuxiàn Gōngsī (Yóuzhèng Biānmǎ：656850). Liánxì Diànhuà：55588723. Diànzǐ Yóuxiāng：icomw@syazfvhd.biz.cn

Bao Quan Kan, Hui Pei Corporation, 730 Sheng Zhi Road, Miyun District, Beijing, China. Postal Code: 656850. Phone Number：55588723. E-mail：icomw@syazfvhd.biz.cn

57。姓名: 包帆铁

住址（广场）：中国北京市西城区柱咚路 249 号淹维广场（邮政编码：262443）。联系电话：15251785。电子邮箱：mjwfk@gieomhjr.squares.cn

Zhù zhǐ: Bāo Fān Tiě Zhōng Guó Běijīng Shì Xī Chéng Qū Zhù Dōng Lù 249 Hào Yān Wéi Guǎng Chǎng (Yóuzhèng Biānmǎ：262443). Liánxì Diànhuà：15251785. Diànzǐ Yóuxiāng：mjwfk@gieomhjr.squares.cn

Fan Tie Bao, Yan Wei Square, 249 Zhu Dong Road, Xicheng District, Beijing, China. Postal Code: 262443. Phone Number：15251785. E-mail：mjwfk@gieomhjr.squares.cn

58。姓名: 宿世人

住址（公共汽车站）：中国北京市昌平区队洵路 689 号红原站（邮政编码：723111）。联系电话：60410209。电子邮箱：tqaux@eklojrvh.transport.cn

Zhù zhǐ: Sù Shì Rén Zhōng Guó Běijīng Shì Chāngpíng Qū Duì Xún Lù 689 Hào Hóng Yuán Zhàn (Yóuzhèng Biānmǎ：723111). Liánxì Diànhuà：60410209. Diànzǐ Yóuxiāng：tqaux@eklojrvh.transport.cn

Shi Ren Su, Hong Yuan Bus Station, 689 Dui Xun Road, Changping District, Beijing, China. Postal Code: 723111. Phone Number：60410209. E-mail：tqaux@eklojrvh.transport.cn

59。姓名：陈兆轶

住址（公司）：中国北京市顺义区学桥路 748 号兵懂有限公司（邮政编码：179650）。联系电话：62568181。电子邮箱：iloda@woufxviq.biz.cn

Zhù zhǐ: Chén Zhào Yì Zhōng Guó Běijīng Shì Shùnyì Qū Xué Qiáo Lù 748 Hào Bīng Dǒng Yǒuxiàn Gōngsī (Yóuzhèng Biānmǎ：179650). Liánxì Diànhuà：62568181. Diànzǐ Yóuxiāng：iloda@woufxviq.biz.cn

Zhao Yi Chen, Bing Dong Corporation, 748 Xue Qiao Road, Shunyi District, Beijing, China. Postal Code: 179650. Phone Number：62568181. E-mail：iloda@woufxviq.biz.cn

60。姓名：毛宽亭

住址（公共汽车站）：中国北京市昌平区俊豹路 148 号熔轼站（邮政编码：478675）。联系电话：97108841。电子邮箱：ghato@pjueczkd.transport.cn

Zhù zhǐ: Máo Kuān Tíng Zhōng Guó Běijīng Shì Chāngpíng Qū Jùn Bào Lù 148 Hào Róng Shì Zhàn (Yóuzhèng Biānmǎ：478675). Liánxì Diànhuà：97108841. Diànzǐ Yóuxiāng：ghato@pjueczkd.transport.cn

Kuan Ting Mao, Rong Shi Bus Station, 148 Jun Bao Road, Changping District, Beijing, China. Postal Code: 478675. Phone Number：97108841. E-mail：ghato@pjueczkd.transport.cn

CHAPTER 3: NAME, SURNAME & ADDRESSES (61-90)

61。姓名: 巢白亭

住址（博物院）：中国北京市怀柔区柱智路 745 号北京博物馆（邮政编码：159639）。联系电话：12992362。电子邮箱：zsugm@nexhwvdm.museums.cn

Zhù zhǐ: Cháo Bái Tíng Zhōng Guó Běijīng Shì Huáiróu Qū Zhù Zhì Lù 745 Hào Běijīng Bó Wù Guǎn (Yóuzhèng Biānmǎ：159639). Liánxì Diànhuà：12992362. Diànzǐ Yóuxiāng：zsugm@nexhwvdm.museums.cn

Bai Ting Chao, Beijing Museum, 745 Zhu Zhi Road, Huairou District, Beijing, China. Postal Code: 159639. Phone Number：12992362. E-mail：zsugm@nexhwvdm.museums.cn

62。姓名: 梁骥宝

住址（家庭）：中国北京市西城区亚化路 268 号晗焯公寓 50 层 102 室（邮政编码：741037）。联系电话：33154394。电子邮箱：vareq@basuzmyl.cn

Zhù zhǐ: Liáng Jì Bǎo Zhōng Guó Běijīng Shì Xī Chéng Qū Yà Huà Lù 268 Hào Hán Zhuō Gōng Yù 50 Céng 102 Shì (Yóuzhèng Biānmǎ：741037). Liánxì Diànhuà：33154394. Diànzǐ Yóuxiāng：vareq@basuzmyl.cn

Ji Bao Liang, Room# 102, Floor# 50, Han Zhuo Apartment, 268 Ya Hua Road, Xicheng District, Beijing, China. Postal Code: 741037. Phone Number：33154394. E-mail：vareq@basuzmyl.cn

63。姓名: 岑毅乐

住址（家庭）：中国北京市平谷区坚守路 803 号翼沛公寓 23 层 918 室（邮政编码：823218）。联系电话：67252641。电子邮箱：gmcws@uspkgnzr.cn

Zhù zhǐ: Cén Yì Lè Zhōng Guó Běijīng Shì Pínggǔ Qū Jiān Shǒu Lù 803 Hào Yì Bèi Gōng Yù 23 Céng 918 Shì (Yóuzhèng Biānmǎ：823218). Liánxì Diànhuà：67252641. Diànzǐ Yóuxiāng：gmcws@uspkgnzr.cn

Yi Le Cen, Room# 918, Floor# 23, Yi Bei Apartment, 803 Jian Shou Road, Pinggu District, Beijing, China. Postal Code: 823218. Phone Number：67252641. E-mail：gmcws@uspkgnzr.cn

64。姓名: 公孙跃世

住址（医院）：中国北京市海淀区立德路 668 号泽山医院（邮政编码：488741）。联系电话：22381609。电子邮箱：omucn@opthasre.health.cn

Zhù zhǐ: Gōngsūn Yuè Shì Zhōng Guó Běijīng Shì Hǎidiàn Qū Lì Dé Lù 668 Hào Zé Shān Yī Yuàn（Yóuzhèng Biānmǎ：488741）. Liánxì Diànhuà：22381609. Diànzǐ Yóuxiāng：omucn@opthasre.health.cn

Yue Shi Gongsun, Ze Shan Hospital, 668 Li De Road, Haidian District, Beijing, China. Postal Code: 488741. Phone Number：22381609. E-mail：omucn@opthasre.health.cn

65。姓名: 臧仓员

住址（酒店）：中国北京市朝阳区强愈路 993 号红强酒店（邮政编码：745091）。联系电话：82112396。电子邮箱：egywv@tjcigqho.biz.cn

Zhù zhǐ: Zāng Cāng Yún Zhōng Guó Běijīng Shì Zhāoyáng Qū Qiǎng Yù Lù 993 Hào Hóng Qiǎng Jiǔ Diàn（Yóuzhèng Biānmǎ：745091）. Liánxì Diànhuà：82112396. Diànzǐ Yóuxiāng：egywv@tjcigqho.biz.cn

Cang Yun Zang, Hong Qiang Hotel, 993 Qiang Yu Road, Chaoyang District, Beijing, China. Postal Code: 745091. Phone Number：82112396. E-mail：egywv@tjcigqho.biz.cn

66。姓名: 上官秀其

住址（公园）：中国北京市朝阳区葆亮路 403 号祥大公园（邮政编码：667367）。联系电话：53676618。电子邮箱：ituzn@whnmlcib.parks.cn

Zhù zhǐ: Shàngguān Xiù Qí Zhōng Guó Běijīng Shì Zhāoyáng Qū Bǎo Liàng Lù 403 Hào Xiáng Dà Gōng Yuán (Yóuzhèng Biānmǎ：667367). Liánxì Diànhuà：53676618. Diànzǐ Yóuxiāng：ituzn@whnmlcib.parks.cn

Xiu Qi Shangguan, Xiang Da Park, 403 Bao Liang Road, Chaoyang District, Beijing, China. Postal Code: 667367. Phone Number：53676618. E-mail：ituzn@whnmlcib.parks.cn

67。姓名: 席其嘉

住址（大学）：中国北京市密云区禹食大学寰游路 927 号（邮政编码：758537）。联系电话：18098933。电子邮箱：pnmrl@xkfmietv.edu.cn

Zhù zhǐ: Xí Qí Jiā Zhōng Guó Běijīng Shì Mìyún Qū Yǔ Shí DàxuéHuán Yóu Lù 927 Hào (Yóuzhèng Biānmǎ：758537). Liánxì Diànhuà：18098933. Diànzǐ Yóuxiāng：pnmrl@xkfmietv.edu.cn

Qi Jia Xi, Yu Shi University, 927 Huan You Road, Miyun District, Beijing, China. Postal Code: 758537. Phone Number：18098933. E-mail：pnmrl@xkfmietv.edu.cn

68。姓名: 卞钊员

住址（公司）：中国北京市延庆区维友路 217 号宽豹有限公司（邮政编码：471174）。联系电话：21225561。电子邮箱：jhrnu@cogwlypt.biz.cn

Zhù zhǐ: Biàn Zhāo Yuán Zhōng Guó Běijīng Shì Yánqìng Qū Wéi Yǒu Lù 217 Hào Kuān Bào Yǒuxiàn Gōngsī (Yóuzhèng Biānmǎ：471174). Liánxì Diànhuà：21225561. Diànzǐ Yóuxiāng：jhrnu@cogwlypt.biz.cn

Zhao Yuan Bian, Kuan Bao Corporation, 217 Wei You Road, Yanqing District, Beijing, China. Postal Code: 471174. Phone Number：21225561. E-mail：jhrnu@cogwlypt.biz.cn

69。姓名: 蓟刚晖

住址（湖泊）：中国北京市顺义区民泽路 725 号可澜湖（邮政编码：674934）。联系电话：97137699。电子邮箱：lrovq@xtralvpb.lakes.cn

Zhù zhǐ: Jì Gāng Huī Zhōng Guó Běijīng Shì Shùnyì Qū Mín Zé Lù 725 Hào Kě Lán Hú (Yóuzhèng Biānmǎ：674934). Liánxì Diànhuà：97137699. Diànzǐ Yóuxiāng：lrovq@xtralvpb.lakes.cn

Gang Hui Ji, Ke Lan Lake, 725 Min Ze Road, Shunyi District, Beijing, China. Postal Code: 674934. Phone Number：97137699. E-mail：lrovq@xtralvpb.lakes.cn

70。姓名: 荣葆鹤

住址（寺庙）：中国北京市石景山区宽亚路 744 号仓祥寺（邮政编码：548810）。联系电话：51464695。电子邮箱：ubihw@cfrsweyp.god.cn

Zhù zhǐ: Róng Bǎo Hè Zhōng Guó Běijīng Shì Shíjǐngshān Qū Kuān Yà Lù 744 Hào Cāng Xiáng Sì (Yóuzhèng Biānmǎ：548810). Liánxì Diànhuà：51464695. Diànzǐ Yóuxiāng：ubihw@cfrsweyp.god.cn

Bao He Rong, Cang Xiang Temple, 744 Kuan Ya Road, Shijingshan District, Beijing, China. Postal Code: 548810. Phone Number：51464695. E-mail：ubihw@cfrsweyp.god.cn

71。姓名: 扶寰勇

住址（大学）：中国北京市密云区顺豪大学员辙路 586 号（邮政编码：538859）。联系电话：29180138。电子邮箱：xizav@uywkqvcg.edu.cn

Zhù zhǐ: Fú Huán Yǒng Zhōng Guó Běijīng Shì Mìyún Qū Shùn Háo DàxuéYún Zhé Lù 586 Hào (Yóuzhèng Biānmǎ：538859). Liánxì Diànhuà：29180138. Diànzǐ Yóuxiāng：xizav@uywkqvcg.edu.cn

Huan Yong Fu, Shun Hao University, 586 Yun Zhe Road, Miyun District, Beijing, China. Postal Code: 538859. Phone Number：29180138. E-mail：xizav@uywkqvcg.edu.cn

72。姓名: 翟兆祥

住址（大学）：中国北京市昌平区伦轶大学坡启路 662 号（邮政编码：494749）。联系电话：18846294。电子邮箱：wtzmu@xklirsmy.edu.cn

Zhù zhǐ: Zhái Zhào Xiáng Zhōng Guó Běijīng Shì Chāngpíng Qū Lún Yì DàxuéPō Qǐ Lù 662 Hào (Yóuzhèng Biānmǎ：494749). Liánxì Diànhuà：18846294. Diànzǐ Yóuxiāng：wtzmu@xklirsmy.edu.cn

Zhao Xiang Zhai, Lun Yi University, 662 Po Qi Road, Changping District, Beijing, China. Postal Code: 494749. Phone Number：18846294. E-mail：wtzmu@xklirsmy.edu.cn

73。姓名: 茅自刚

住址（火车站）：中国北京市大兴区化禹路 229 号北京站（邮政编码：213407）。联系电话：14911345。电子邮箱：nudeg@hqzwpdrf.chr.cn

Zhù zhǐ: Máo Zì Gāng Zhōng Guó Běijīng Shì Dàxīng Qū Huā Yǔ Lù 229 Hào Běijīng Zhàn (Yóuzhèng Biānmǎ：213407). Liánxì Diànhuà：14911345. Diànzǐ Yóuxiāng：nudeg@hqzwpdrf.chr.cn

Zi Gang Mao, Beijing Railway Station, 229 Hua Yu Road, Daxing District, Beijing, China. Postal Code: 213407. Phone Number：14911345. E-mail：nudeg@hqzwpdrf.chr.cn

74。姓名: 窦易振

住址（寺庙）：中国北京市密云区人宝路 377 号际跃寺（邮政编码：858562）。联系电话：16592697。电子邮箱：fmpdb@lvnhrftm.god.cn

Zhù zhǐ: Dòu Yì Zhèn Zhōng Guó Běijīng Shì Mìyún Qū Rén Bǎo Lù 377 Hào Jì Yuè Sì (Yóuzhèng Biānmǎ：858562). Liánxì Diànhuà：16592697. Diànzǐ Yóuxiāng：fmpdb@lvnhrftm.god.cn

Yi Zhen Dou, Ji Yue Temple, 377 Ren Bao Road, Miyun District, Beijing, China. Postal Code: 858562. Phone Number：16592697. E-mail：fmpdb@lvnhrftm.god.cn

75。姓名: 贝恩勇

住址（湖泊）：中国北京市延庆区进辉路 940 号钢征湖（邮政编码：842061）。联系电话：34023608。电子邮箱：avlwt@nhrcafpq.lakes.cn

Zhù zhǐ: Bèi Ēn Yǒng Zhōng Guó Běijīng Shì Yánqìng Qū Jìn Huī Lù 940 Hào Gāng Zhēng Hú（Yóuzhèng Biānmǎ：842061). Liánxì Diànhuà：34023608. Diànzǐ Yóuxiāng：avlwt@nhrcafpq.lakes.cn

En Yong Bei, Gang Zheng Lake, 940 Jin Hui Road, Yanqing District, Beijing, China. Postal Code: 842061. Phone Number：34023608. E-mail：avlwt@nhrcafpq.lakes.cn

76。姓名: 周敬葆

住址（酒店）：中国北京市密云区坤翰路 204 号敬柱酒店（邮政编码：449000）。联系电话：23499468。电子邮箱：triaw@vntclueh.biz.cn

Zhù zhǐ: Zhōu Jìng Bǎo Zhōng Guó Běijīng Shì Mìyún Qū Kūn Hàn Lù 204 Hào Jìng Zhù Jiǔ Diàn（Yóuzhèng Biānmǎ：449000). Liánxì Diànhuà：23499468. Diànzǐ Yóuxiāng：triaw@vntclueh.biz.cn

Jing Bao Zhou, Jing Zhu Hotel, 204 Kun Han Road, Miyun District, Beijing, China. Postal Code: 449000. Phone Number：23499468. E-mail：triaw@vntclueh.biz.cn

77。姓名: 申大冕

住址（大学）：中国北京市延庆区威国大学领波路 803 号（邮政编码：412182）。联系电话：21408818。电子邮箱：dbjou@hdtmekjg.edu.cn

Zhù zhǐ: Shēn Dà Miǎn Zhōng Guó Běijīng Shì Yánqìng Qū Wēi Guó DàxuéLǐng Bō Lù 803 Hào（Yóuzhèng Biānmǎ：412182). Liánxì Diànhuà：21408818. Diànzǐ Yóuxiāng：dbjou@hdtmekjg.edu.cn

Da Mian Shen, Wei Guo University, 803 Ling Bo Road, Yanqing District, Beijing, China. Postal Code: 412182. Phone Number：21408818. E-mail：dbjou@hdtmekjg.edu.cn

78。姓名: 鲍龙帆

住址（酒店）：中国北京市东城区翰全路 770 号伦立酒店（邮政编码：551693）。联系电话：71822780。电子邮箱：csdvl@fsonvbjk.biz.cn

Zhù zhǐ: Bào Lóng Fān Zhōng Guó Běijīng Shì Dōng Chéng Qū Hàn Quán Lù 770 Hào Lún Lì Jiǔ Diàn（Yóuzhèng Biānmǎ：551693). Liánxì Diànhuà：71822780. Diànzǐ Yóuxiāng：csdvl@fsonvbjk.biz.cn

Long Fan Bao, Lun Li Hotel, 770 Han Quan Road, Dongcheng Area, Beijing, China. Postal Code: 551693. Phone Number：71822780. E-mail：csdvl@fsonvbjk.biz.cn

79。姓名: 谈智院

住址（公司）：中国北京市平谷区斌鹤路 818 号队可有限公司（邮政编码：926804）。联系电话：58757970。电子邮箱：upoja@utywzsxb.biz.cn

Zhù zhǐ: Tán Zhì Yuàn Zhōng Guó Běijīng Shì Pínggǔ Qū Bīn Hè Lù 818 Hào Duì Kě Yǒuxiàn Gōngsī（Yóuzhèng Biānmǎ：926804). Liánxì Diànhuà：58757970. Diànzǐ Yóuxiāng：upoja@utywzsxb.biz.cn

Zhi Yuan Tan, Dui Ke Corporation, 818 Bin He Road, Pinggu District, Beijing, China. Postal Code: 926804. Phone Number：58757970. E-mail：upoja@utywzsxb.biz.cn

80。姓名: 喻禹世

住址（酒店）：中国北京市延庆区陶成路 503 号石冕酒店（邮政编码：779420）。联系电话：58165034。电子邮箱：pkubg@yjsdbwlp.biz.cn

Zhù zhǐ: Yù Yǔ Shì Zhōng Guó Běijīng Shì Yánqìng Qū Táo Chéng Lù 503 Hào Dàn Miǎn Jiǔ Diàn（Yóuzhèng Biānmǎ：779420). Liánxì Diànhuà：58165034. Diànzǐ Yóuxiāng：pkubg@yjsdbwlp.biz.cn

Yu Shi Yu, Dan Mian Hotel, 503 Tao Cheng Road, Yanqing District, Beijing, China. Postal Code: 779420. Phone Number：58165034. E-mail：pkubg@yjsdbwlp.biz.cn

81。姓名: 仲沛福

住址（火车站）：中国北京市门头沟区山翼路 453 号北京站（邮政编码：114362）。联系电话：66158598。电子邮箱：btxer@jhegitxw.chr.cn

Zhù zhǐ: Zhòng Bèi Fú Zhōng Guó Běijīng Shì Méntóugōu Qū Shān Yì Lù 453 Hào Běijīng Zhàn（Yóuzhèng Biānmǎ：114362). Liánxì Diànhuà：66158598. Diànzǐ Yóuxiāng：btxer@jhegitxw.chr.cn

Bei Fu Zhong, Beijing Railway Station, 453 Shan Yi Road, Mentougou District, Beijing, China. Postal Code: 114362. Phone Number：66158598. E-mail：btxer@jhegitxw.chr.cn

82。姓名: 从泽骥

住址（博物院）：中国北京市西城区九渊路 321 号北京博物馆（邮政编码：945146）。联系电话：23318275。电子邮箱：zsedk@nqmbkihs.museums.cn

Zhù zhǐ: Cóng Zé Jì Zhōng Guó Běijīng Shì Xī Chéng Qū Jiǔ Yuān Lù 321 Hào Běijīng Bó Wù Guǎn（Yóuzhèng Biānmǎ：945146). Liánxì Diànhuà：23318275. Diànzǐ Yóuxiāng：zsedk@nqmbkihs.museums.cn

Ze Ji Cong, Beijing Museum, 321 Jiu Yuan Road, Xicheng District, Beijing, China. Postal Code: 945146. Phone Number：23318275. E-mail：zsedk@nqmbkihs.museums.cn

83。姓名：常进德

住址（公共汽车站）：中国北京市东城区澜祥路 694 号盛源站（邮政编码：810115）。联系电话：40793969。电子邮箱：rqdmh@bxluzvkm.transport.cn

Zhù zhǐ: Cháng Jìn Dé Zhōng Guó Běijīng Shì Dōng Chéng Qū Lán Xiáng Lù 694 Hào Shèng Yuán Zhàn（Yóuzhèng Biānmǎ：810115). Liánxì Diànhuà：40793969. Diànzǐ Yóuxiāng：rqdmh@bxluzvkm.transport.cn

Jin De Chang, Sheng Yuan Bus Station, 694 Lan Xiang Road, Dongcheng Area, Beijing, China. Postal Code: 810115. Phone Number：40793969. E-mail：rqdmh@bxluzvkm.transport.cn

84。姓名：许鸣继

住址（公园）：中国北京市顺义区淹坤路 785 号居翼公园（邮政编码：425796）。联系电话：69113791。电子邮箱：dhavw@wrbjeoyn.parks.cn

Zhù zhǐ: Xǔ Míng Jì Zhōng Guó Běijīng Shì Shùnyì Qū Yān Kūn Lù 785 Hào Jū Yì Gōng Yuán（Yóuzhèng Biānmǎ：425796). Liánxì Diànhuà：69113791. Diànzǐ Yóuxiāng：dhavw@wrbjeoyn.parks.cn

Ming Ji Xu, Ju Yi Park, 785 Yan Kun Road, Shunyi District, Beijing, China. Postal Code: 425796. Phone Number：69113791. E-mail：dhavw@wrbjeoyn.parks.cn

85。姓名：左盛征

住址（机场）：中国北京市海淀区乙立路 303 号北京学亚国际机场（邮政编码：341063）。联系电话：78204348。电子邮箱：lkhiq@caqifxmh.airports.cn

Zhù zhǐ: Zuǒ Chéng Zhēng Zhōng Guó Běijīng Shì Hǎidiàn Qū Yǐ Lì Lù 303 Hào Běijīng Xué Yà Guó Jì Jī Chǎng（Yóuzhèng Biānmǎ：341063). Liánxì Diànhuà：78204348. Diànzǐ Yóuxiāng：lkhiq@caqifxmh.airports.cn

Cheng Zheng Zuo, Beijing Xue Ya International Airport, 303 Yi Li Road, Haidian District, Beijing, China. Postal Code: 341063. Phone Number：78204348. E-mail：lkhiq@caqifxmh.airports.cn

86。姓名: 秋庆白

住址（酒店）：中国北京市海淀区鸣石路 960 号泽胜酒店（邮政编码：398578）。联系电话：65221413。电子邮箱：huwqc@phvbxisl.biz.cn

Zhù zhǐ: Qiū Qìng Bái Zhōng Guó Běijīng Shì Hǎidiàn Qū Míng Shí Lù 960 Hào Zé Shēng Jiǔ Diàn（Yóuzhèng Biānmǎ：398578). Liánxì Diànhuà：65221413. Diànzǐ Yóuxiāng：huwqc@phvbxisl.biz.cn

Qing Bai Qiu, Ze Sheng Hotel, 960 Ming Shi Road, Haidian District, Beijing, China. Postal Code: 398578. Phone Number：65221413. E-mail：huwqc@phvbxisl.biz.cn

87。姓名: 廖洵铭

住址（公园）：中国北京市海淀区兵独路 703 号熔葛公园（邮政编码：948146）。联系电话：73298225。电子邮箱：fizmo@wdnlckxp.parks.cn

Zhù zhǐ: Liào Xún Míng Zhōng Guó Běijīng Shì Hǎidiàn Qū Bīng Dú Lù 703 Hào Róng Gé Gōng Yuán（Yóuzhèng Biānmǎ：948146). Liánxì Diànhuà：73298225. Diànzǐ Yóuxiāng：fizmo@wdnlckxp.parks.cn

Xun Ming Liao, Rong Ge Park, 703 Bing Du Road, Haidian District, Beijing, China. Postal Code: 948146. Phone Number：73298225. E-mail：fizmo@wdnlckxp.parks.cn

88。姓名: 阳王兆

住址（公共汽车站）：中国北京市大兴区翰俊路 485 号锡坚站（邮政编码：334542）。联系电话：89594802。电子邮箱：dzlet@quyboirx.transport.cn

Zhù zhǐ: Yáng Wáng Zhào Zhōng Guó Běijīng Shì Dàxīng Qū Hàn Jùn Lù 485 Hào Xī Jiān Zhàn (Yóuzhèng Biānmǎ：334542). Liánxì Diànhuà：89594802. Diànzǐ Yóuxiāng：dzlet@quyboirx.transport.cn

Wang Zhao Yang, Xi Jian Bus Station, 485 Han Jun Road, Daxing District, Beijing, China. Postal Code: 334542. Phone Number：89594802. E-mail：dzlet@quyboirx.transport.cn

89。姓名: 秋磊宝

住址（博物院）：中国北京市石景山区辙沛路 416 号北京博物馆（邮政编码：497288）。联系电话：25137330。电子邮箱：gqdbo@twnmdyhl.museums.cn

Zhù zhǐ: Qiū Lěi Bǎo Zhōng Guó Běijīng Shì Shíjǐngshān Qū Zhé Pèi Lù 416 Hào Běijīng Bó Wù Guǎn (Yóuzhèng Biānmǎ：497288). Liánxì Diànhuà：25137330. Diànzǐ Yóuxiāng：gqdbo@twnmdyhl.museums.cn

Lei Bao Qiu, Beijing Museum, 416 Zhe Pei Road, Shijingshan District, Beijing, China. Postal Code: 497288. Phone Number：25137330. E-mail：gqdbo@twnmdyhl.museums.cn

90。姓名: 仇督世阳

住址（医院）：中国北京市西城区食钊路 927 号先学医院（邮政编码：317762）。联系电话：34672265。电子邮箱：ubhiz@hqtucyfs.health.cn

Zhù zhǐ: Zhǎngdū Shì Yáng Zhōng Guó Běijīng Shì Xī Chéng Qū Shí Zhāo Lù 927 Hào Xiān Xué Yī Yuàn (Yóuzhèng Biānmǎ：317762). Liánxì Diànhuà：34672265. Diànzǐ Yóuxiāng：ubhiz@hqtucyfs.health.cn

Shi Yang Zhangdu, Xian Xue Hospital, 927 Shi Zhao Road, Xicheng District, Beijing, China. Postal Code: 317762. Phone Number：34672265. E-mail：ubhiz@hqtucyfs.health.cn

CHAPTER 4: NAME, SURNAME & ADDRESSES (91-120)

91。姓名: 廉帆敬

住址（医院）：中国北京市顺义区冠谢路 858 号石陆医院（邮政编码：421019）。联系电话：62768588。电子邮箱：qscoz@nzgarycq.health.cn

Zhù zhǐ: Lián Fān Jìng Zhōng Guó Běijīng Shì Shùnyì Qū Guàn Xiè Lù 858 Hào Shí Liù Yī Yuàn (Yóuzhèng Biānmǎ: 421019). Liánxì Diànhuà: 62768588. Diànzǐ Yóuxiāng：qscoz@nzgarycq.health.cn

Fan Jing Lian, Shi Liu Hospital, 858 Guan Xie Road, Shunyi District, Beijing, China. Postal Code: 421019. Phone Number：62768588. E-mail：qscoz@nzgarycq.health.cn

92。姓名: 刘轼乙

住址（博物院）：中国北京市海淀区冠红路 882 号北京博物馆（邮政编码：911088）。联系电话：34552028。电子邮箱：qrjhy@brhejydp.museums.cn

Zhù zhǐ: Liú Shì Yǐ Zhōng Guó Běijīng Shì Hǎidiàn Qū Guàn Hóng Lù 882 Hào Běijīng Bó Wù Guǎn (Yóuzhèng Biānmǎ: 911088). Liánxì Diànhuà: 34552028. Diànzǐ Yóuxiāng：qrjhy@brhejydp.museums.cn

Shi Yi Liu, Beijing Museum, 882 Guan Hong Road, Haidian District, Beijing, China. Postal Code: 911088. Phone Number：34552028. E-mail：qrjhy@brhejydp.museums.cn

93。姓名: 权陶勇

住址（寺庙）：中国北京市西城区波盛路 248 号珂克寺（邮政编码：129342）。联系电话：24791175。电子邮箱：gdqvm@shwoxqlk.god.cn

Zhù zhǐ: Quán Táo Yǒng Zhōng Guó Běijīng Shì Xī Chéng Qū Bō Chéng Lù 248 Hào Kē Kè Sì (Yóuzhèng Biānmǎ: 129342). Liánxì Diànhuà: 24791175. Diànzǐ Yóuxiāng：gdqvm@shwoxqlk.god.cn

Tao Yong Quan, Ke Ke Temple, 248 Bo Cheng Road, Xicheng District, Beijing, China. Postal Code: 129342. Phone Number：24791175. E-mail：gdqvm@shwoxqlk.god.cn

94。姓名: 党乙珂

住址（酒店）：中国北京市延庆区澜兆路 356 号九发酒店（邮政编码：113845）。联系电话：50485796。电子邮箱：axlgp@rlmvadnu.biz.cn

Zhù zhǐ: Dǎng Yǐ Kē Zhōng Guó Běijīng Shì Yánqìng Qū Lán Zhào Lù 356 Hào Jiǔ Fā Jiǔ Diàn（Yóuzhèng Biānmǎ：113845). Liánxì Diànhuà：50485796. Diànzǐ Yóuxiāng：axlgp@rlmvadnu.biz.cn

Yi Ke Dang, Jiu Fa Hotel, 356 Lan Zhao Road, Yanqing District, Beijing, China. Postal Code: 113845. Phone Number：50485796. E-mail：axlgp@rlmvadnu.biz.cn

95。姓名: 蓝可独

住址（湖泊）：中国北京市丰台区洵辉路 299 号化来湖（邮政编码：442245）。联系电话：91380637。电子邮箱：hvomu@zsibjqac.lakes.cn

Zhù zhǐ: Lán Kě Dú Zhōng Guó Běijīng Shì Fēngtái Qū Xún Huī Lù 299 Hào Huā Lái Hú（Yóuzhèng Biānmǎ：442245). Liánxì Diànhuà：91380637. Diànzǐ Yóuxiāng：hvomu@zsibjqac.lakes.cn

Ke Du Lan, Hua Lai Lake, 299 Xun Hui Road, Fengtai District, Beijing, China. Postal Code: 442245. Phone Number：91380637. E-mail：hvomu@zsibjqac.lakes.cn

96。姓名: 逯辉先

住址（火车站）：中国北京市门头沟区沛振路 164 号北京站（邮政编码：356138）。联系电话：83028373。电子邮箱：vcbzu@kzsulrwx.chr.cn

Zhù zhǐ: Lù Huī Xiān Zhōng Guó Běijīng Shì Méntóugōu Qū Bèi Zhèn Lù 164 Hào Běijīng Zhàn（Yóuzhèng Biānmǎ：356138). Liánxì Diànhuà：83028373. Diànzǐ Yóuxiāng：vcbzu@kzsulrwx.chr.cn

Hui Xian Lu, Beijing Railway Station, 164 Bei Zhen Road, Mentougou District, Beijing, China. Postal Code: 356138. Phone Number：83028373. E-mail：vcbzu@kzsulrwx.chr.cn

97。姓名: 佟山珏

住址（机场）：中国北京市密云区征翰路 446 号北京振舟国际机场（邮政编码：308600）。联系电话：65893246。电子邮箱：utngv@jzburhaw.airports.cn

Zhù zhǐ: Tóng Shān Jué Zhōng Guó Běijīng Shì Mìyún Qū Zhēng Hàn Lù 446 Hào Běijīng Zhèn Zhōu Guó Jì Jī Chǎng（Yóuzhèng Biānmǎ：308600). Liánxì Diànhuà：65893246. Diànzǐ Yóuxiāng：utngv@jzburhaw.airports.cn

Shan Jue Tong, Beijing Zhen Zhou International Airport, 446 Zheng Han Road, Miyun District, Beijing, China. Postal Code: 308600. Phone Number：65893246. E-mail：utngv@jzburhaw.airports.cn

98。姓名: 桂晖译

住址（公园）：中国北京市海淀区金兵路 672 号帆锤公园（邮政编码：395411）。联系电话：46908502。电子邮箱：kpjnu@mcwdsabt.parks.cn

Zhù zhǐ: Guì Huī Yì Zhōng Guó Běijīng Shì Hǎidiàn Qū Jīn Bīng Lù 672 Hào Fān Chuí Gōng Yuán（Yóuzhèng Biānmǎ：395411). Liánxì Diànhuà：46908502. Diànzǐ Yóuxiāng：kpjnu@mcwdsabt.parks.cn

Hui Yi Gui, Fan Chui Park, 672 Jin Bing Road, Haidian District, Beijing, China. Postal Code: 395411. Phone Number：46908502. E-mail：kpjnu@mcwdsabt.parks.cn

99。姓名: 彭王风

住址（寺庙）：中国北京市延庆区大钊路 192 号进超寺（邮政编码：798451）。联系电话：32825434。电子邮箱：dubhr@lsbpihyn.god.cn

Zhù zhǐ: Péng Wáng Fēng Zhōng Guó Běijīng Shì Yánqìng Qū Dà Zhāo Lù 192 Hào Jìn Chāo Sì (Yóuzhèng Biānmǎ: 798451). Liánxì Diànhuà: 32825434. Diànzǐ Yóuxiāng: dubhr@lsbpihyn.god.cn

Wang Feng Peng, Jin Chao Temple, 192 Da Zhao Road, Yanqing District, Beijing, China. Postal Code: 798451. Phone Number: 32825434. E-mail: dubhr@lsbpihyn.god.cn

100。姓名: 左丘彬翰

住址（火车站）：中国北京市顺义区盛光路 134 号北京站 （邮政编码：413890）。联系电话：71817829。电子邮箱：ugcsn@fkhlzmou.chr.cn

Zhù zhǐ: Zuǒqiū Bīn Hàn Zhōng Guó Běijīng Shì Shùnyì Qū Shèng Guāng Lù 134 Hào Běijīng Zhàn (Yóuzhèng Biānmǎ: 413890). Liánxì Diànhuà: 71817829. Diànzǐ Yóuxiāng: ugcsn@fkhlzmou.chr.cn

Bin Han Zuoqiu, Beijing Railway Station, 134 Sheng Guang Road, Shunyi District, Beijing, China. Postal Code: 413890. Phone Number: 71817829. E-mail: ugcsn@fkhlzmou.chr.cn

101。姓名: 南宫波守

住址（公司）：中国北京市大兴区豹民路 959 号学咚有限公司 （邮政编码：777962）。联系电话：32837758。电子邮箱：txoum@rqgxumdz.biz.cn

Zhù zhǐ: Nángōng Bō Shǒu Zhōng Guó Běijīng Shì Dàxīng Qū Bào Mín Lù 959 Hào Xué Dōng Yǒuxiàn Gōngsī (Yóuzhèng Biānmǎ: 777962). Liánxì Diànhuà: 32837758. Diànzǐ Yóuxiāng: txoum@rqgxumdz.biz.cn

Bo Shou Nangong, Xue Dong Corporation, 959 Bao Min Road, Daxing District, Beijing, China. Postal Code: 777962. Phone Number: 32837758. E-mail: txoum@rqgxumdz.biz.cn

102。姓名: 韦坤员

住址（酒店）：中国北京市密云区嘉沛路 491 号山兵酒店（邮政编码：650199）。联系电话：38209086。电子邮箱：mgrak@xjnqswev.biz.cn

Zhù zhǐ: Wéi Kūn Yuán Zhōng Guó Běijīng Shì Mìyún Qū Jiā Bèi Lù 491 Hào Shān Bīng Jiǔ Diàn (Yóuzhèng Biānmǎ: 650199). Liánxì Diànhuà：38209086. Diànzǐ Yóuxiāng：mgrak@xjnqswev.biz.cn

Kun Yuan Wei, Shan Bing Hotel, 491 Jia Bei Road, Miyun District, Beijing, China. Postal Code: 650199. Phone Number：38209086. E-mail：mgrak@xjnqswev.biz.cn

103。姓名: 牛成白

住址（博物院）：中国北京市朝阳区淘愈路 717 号北京博物馆（邮政编码：541307）。联系电话：54992591。电子邮箱：dwvqx@pehnkswb.museums.cn

Zhù zhǐ: Niú Chéng Bái Zhōng Guó Běijīng Shì Zhāoyáng Qū Xún Yù Lù 717 Hào Běijīng Bó Wù Guǎn (Yóuzhèng Biānmǎ: 541307). Liánxì Diànhuà: 54992591. Diànzǐ Yóuxiāng: dwvqx@pehnkswb.museums.cn

Cheng Bai Niu, Beijing Museum, 717 Xun Yu Road, Chaoyang District, Beijing, China. Postal Code: 541307. Phone Number：54992591. E-mail：dwvqx@pehnkswb.museums.cn

104。姓名: 詹波化

住址（公园）：中国北京市大兴区仓迅路 774 号振臻公园（邮政编码：163896）。联系电话：45791205。电子邮箱：dsywh@nrajczph.parks.cn

Zhù zhǐ: Zhān Bō Huà Zhōng Guó Běijīng Shì Dàxīng Qū Cāng Xùn Lù 774 Hào Zhèn Zhēn Gōng Yuán (Yóuzhèng Biānmǎ: 163896). Liánxì Diànhuà: 45791205. Diànzǐ Yóuxiāng: dsywh@nrajczph.parks.cn

Bo Hua Zhan, Zhen Zhen Park, 774 Cang Xun Road, Daxing District, Beijing, China. Postal Code: 163896. Phone Number：45791205. E-mail：dsywh@nrajczph.parks.cn

105。姓名: 司空咚寰

住址（家庭）：中国北京市平谷区迅学路 370 号黎钊公寓 28 层 944 室（邮政编码：783230）。联系电话：55548372。电子邮箱：aqmty@efgrbzxd.cn

Zhù zhǐ: Sīkōng Dōng Huán Zhōng Guó Běijīng Shì Pínggǔ Qū Xùn Xué Lù 370 Hào Lí Zhāo Gōng Yù 28 Céng 944 Shì (Yóuzhèng Biānmǎ：783230). Liánxì Diànhuà：55548372. Diànzǐ Yóuxiāng：aqmty@efgrbzxd.cn

Dong Huan Sikong, Room# 944, Floor# 28, Li Zhao Apartment, 370 Xun Xue Road, Pinggu District, Beijing, China. Postal Code: 783230. Phone Number：55548372. E-mail：aqmty@efgrbzxd.cn

106。姓名: 融石土

住址（公司）：中国北京市大兴区珂茂路 483 号化淹有限公司（邮政编码：250123）。联系电话：11506274。电子邮箱：yfumz@nwhftykv.biz.cn

Zhù zhǐ: Róng Dàn Tǔ Zhōng Guó Běijīng Shì Dàxīng Qū Kē Mào Lù 483 Hào Huà Yān Yǒuxiàn Gōngsī (Yóuzhèng Biānmǎ：250123). Liánxì Diànhuà：11506274. Diànzǐ Yóuxiāng：yfumz@nwhftykv.biz.cn

Dan Tu Rong, Hua Yan Corporation, 483 Ke Mao Road, Daxing District, Beijing, China. Postal Code: 250123. Phone Number：11506274. E-mail：yfumz@nwhftykv.biz.cn

107。姓名: 苗中继

住址（博物院）：中国北京市石景山区晗岐路 312 号北京博物馆（邮政编码：704576）。联系电话：61532387。电子邮箱：jwktf@uhodyscf.museums.cn

Zhù zhǐ: Miáo Zhōng Jì Zhōng Guó Běijīng Shì Shíjǐngshān Qū Hán Qí Lù 312 Hào Běijīng Bó Wù Guǎn (Yóuzhèng Biānmǎ：704576). Liánxì Diànhuà：61532387. Diànzǐ Yóuxiāng：jwktf@uhodyscf.museums.cn

Zhong Ji Miao, Beijing Museum, 312 Han Qi Road, Shijingshan District, Beijing, China. Postal Code: 704576. Phone Number：61532387. E-mail：jwktf@uhodyscf.museums.cn

108。姓名: 爱辙晗

住址（广场）：中国北京市西城区原福路 175 号金胜广场（邮政编码：731670）。联系电话：88237404。电子邮箱：dgvxi@rxoqlkyt.squares.cn

Zhù zhǐ: Ài Zhé Hán Zhōng Guó Běijīng Shì Xī Chéng Qū Yuán Fú Lù 175 Hào Jīn Shēng Guǎng Chǎng （Yóuzhèng Biānmǎ：731670). Liánxì Diànhuà：88237404. Diànzǐ Yóuxiāng：dgvxi@rxoqlkyt.squares.cn

Zhe Han Ai, Jin Sheng Square, 175 Yuan Fu Road, Xicheng District, Beijing, China. Postal Code: 731670. Phone Number：88237404. E-mail：dgvxi@rxoqlkyt.squares.cn

109。姓名: 穆仲茂

住址（湖泊）：中国北京市昌平区守磊路 184 号化惟湖（邮政编码：448273）。联系电话：50911995。电子邮箱：anhej@xorvdyhj.lakes.cn

Zhù zhǐ: Mù Zhòng Mào Zhōng Guó Běijīng Shì Chāngpíng Qū Shǒu Lěi Lù 184 Hào Huà Wéi Hú （Yóuzhèng Biānmǎ：448273). Liánxì Diànhuà：50911995. Diànzǐ Yóuxiāng：anhej@xorvdyhj.lakes.cn

Zhong Mao Mu, Hua Wei Lake, 184 Shou Lei Road, Changping District, Beijing, China. Postal Code: 448273. Phone Number：50911995. E-mail：anhej@xorvdyhj.lakes.cn

110。姓名: 郁人石

住址（机场）：中国北京市石景山区辙大路 776 号北京晖冠国际机场（邮政编码：562346）。联系电话：74542127。电子邮箱：jidrw@mwqtlvpn.airports.cn

Zhù zhǐ: Yù Rén Shí Zhōng Guó Běijīng Shì Shíjǐngshān Qū Zhé Dà Lù 776 Hào Běijīng Huī Guàn Guó Jì Jī Chǎng（Yóuzhèng Biānmǎ：562346). Liánxì Diànhuà：74542127. Diànzǐ Yóuxiāng：jidrw@mwqtlvpn.airports.cn

Ren Shi Yu, Beijing Hui Guan International Airport, 776 Zhe Da Road, Shijingshan District, Beijing, China. Postal Code: 562346. Phone Number：74542127. E-mail：jidrw@mwqtlvpn.airports.cn

111。姓名: 莘楚彬

住址（湖泊）：中国北京市昌平区启王路 679 号臻龙湖（邮政编码：668538）。联系电话：66254469。电子邮箱：xgjqd@lxeyghow.lakes.cn

Zhù zhǐ: Shēn Chǔ Bīn Zhōng Guó Běijīng Shì Chāngpíng Qū Qǐ Wàng Lù 679 Hào Zhēn Lóng Hú（Yóuzhèng Biānmǎ：668538). Liánxì Diànhuà：66254469. Diànzǐ Yóuxiāng：xgjqd@lxeyghow.lakes.cn

Chu Bin Shen, Zhen Long Lake, 679 Qi Wang Road, Changping District, Beijing, China. Postal Code: 668538. Phone Number：66254469. E-mail：xgjqd@lxeyghow.lakes.cn

112。姓名: 微晗谢

住址（酒店）：中国北京市东城区其斌路 451 号仓锤酒店（邮政编码：515284）。联系电话：51358074。电子邮箱：bxmwp@aywslbme.biz.cn

Zhù zhǐ: Wēi Hán Xiè Zhōng Guó Běijīng Shì Dōng Chéng Qū Qí Bīn Lù 451 Hào Cāng Chuí Jiǔ Diàn（Yóuzhèng Biānmǎ：515284). Liánxì Diànhuà：51358074. Diànzǐ Yóuxiāng：bxmwp@aywslbme.biz.cn

Han Xie Wei, Cang Chui Hotel, 451 Qi Bin Road, Dongcheng Area, Beijing, China. Postal Code: 515284. Phone Number：51358074. E-mail：bxmwp@aywslbme.biz.cn

113。姓名: 闾丘珏人

住址（机场）：中国北京市顺义区伦星路 932 号北京强铁国际机场（邮政编码：807863）。联系电话：90336891。电子邮箱：bhlqu@lnkxyuch.airports.cn

Zhù zhǐ: Lǚqiū Jué Rén Zhōng Guó Běijīng Shì Shùnyì Qū Lún Xīng Lù 932 Hào Běijīng Qiǎng Tiě Guó Jì Jī Chǎng（Yóuzhèng Biānmǎ：807863). Liánxì Diànhuà：90336891. Diànzǐ Yóuxiāng：bhlqu@lnkxyuch.airports.cn

Jue Ren Llvqu, Beijing Qiang Tie International Airport, 932 Lun Xing Road, Shunyi District, Beijing, China. Postal Code: 807863. Phone Number：90336891. E-mail：bhlqu@lnkxyuch.airports.cn

114。姓名: 万俟晗宝

住址（公共汽车站）：中国北京市平谷区易炯路 616 号舟汉站（邮政编码：869905）。联系电话：68213503。电子邮箱：dcyae@jusmgptk.transport.cn

Zhù zhǐ: Mòqí Hán Bǎo Zhōng Guó Běijīng Shì Pínggǔ Qū Yì Jiǒng Lù 616 Hào Zhōu Hàn Zhàn（Yóuzhèng Biānmǎ：869905). Liánxì Diànhuà：68213503. Diànzǐ Yóuxiāng：dcyae@jusmgptk.transport.cn

Han Bao Moqi, Zhou Han Bus Station, 616 Yi Jiong Road, Pinggu District, Beijing, China. Postal Code: 869905. Phone Number：68213503. E-mail：dcyae@jusmgptk.transport.cn

115。姓名: 申屠启顺

住址（寺庙）：中国北京市昌平区葛立路 342 号钢辙寺（邮政编码：949683）。联系电话：28622829。电子邮箱：scwdi@myqbnset.god.cn

Zhù zhǐ: Shēntú Qǐ Shùn Zhōng Guó Běijīng Shì Chāngpíng Qū Gé Lì Lù 342 Hào Gāng Zhé Sì（Yóuzhèng Biānmǎ：949683). Liánxì Diànhuà：28622829. Diànzǐ Yóuxiāng：scwdi@myqbnset.god.cn

Qi Shun Shentu, Gang Zhe Temple, 342 Ge Li Road, Changping District, Beijing, China. Postal Code: 949683. Phone Number：28622829. E-mail：scwdi@myqbnset.god.cn

116。姓名: 邬汉亚

住址（家庭）：中国北京市东城区翰己路 730 号全臻公寓 8 层 289 室（邮政编码：771829）。联系电话：22180765。电子邮箱：hnkua@kjewlcha.cn

Zhù zhǐ: Wū Hàn Yà Zhōng Guó Běijīng Shì Dōng Chéng Qū Hàn Jǐ Lù 730 Hào Quán Zhēn Gōng Yù 8 Céng 289 Shì (Yóuzhèng Biānmǎ：771829). Liánxì Diànhuà：22180765. Diànzǐ Yóuxiāng：hnkua@kjewlcha.cn

Han Ya Wu, Room# 289, Floor# 8, Quan Zhen Apartment, 730 Han Ji Road, Dongcheng Area, Beijing, China. Postal Code: 771829. Phone Number：22180765. E-mail：hnkua@kjewlcha.cn

117。姓名: 支稼钊

住址（酒店）：中国北京市昌平区白伦路 599 号彬大酒店（邮政编码：937374）。联系电话：48210230。电子邮箱：xhnca@dzgwhjxe.biz.cn

Zhù zhǐ: Zhī Jià Zhāo Zhōng Guó Běijīng Shì Chāngpíng Qū Bái Lún Lù 599 Hào Bīn Dài Jiǔ Diàn (Yóuzhèng Biānmǎ：937374). Liánxì Diànhuà：48210230. Diànzǐ Yóuxiāng：xhnca@dzgwhjxe.biz.cn

Jia Zhao Zhi, Bin Dai Hotel, 599 Bai Lun Road, Changping District, Beijing, China. Postal Code: 937374. Phone Number：48210230. E-mail：xhnca@dzgwhjxe.biz.cn

118。姓名: 蔚焯豪

住址（机场）：中国北京市怀柔区可可路 884 号北京兆涛国际机场（邮政编码：774615）。联系电话：96231480。电子邮箱：rqcfo@agfdhnqr.airports.cn

Zhù zhǐ: Wèi Chāo Háo Zhōng Guó Běijīng Shì Huáiróu Qū Kě Kě Lù 884 Hào Běijīng Zhào Tāo Guó Jì Jī Chǎng（Yóuzhèng Biānmǎ：774615). Liánxì Diànhuà：96231480. Diànzǐ Yóuxiāng：rqcfo@agfdhnqr.airports.cn

Chao Hao Wei, Beijing Zhao Tao International Airport, 884 Ke Ke Road, Huairou District, Beijing, China. Postal Code: 774615. Phone Number：96231480. E-mail：rqcfo@agfdhnqr.airports.cn

119。姓名: 左丘翰振

住址（医院）：中国北京市顺义区陶谢路 998 号守员医院（邮政编码：337580）。联系电话：55579787。电子邮箱：bdrkh@cylxqmbv.health.cn

Zhù zhǐ: Zuǒqiū Hàn Zhèn Zhōng Guó Běijīng Shì Shùnyì Qū Táo Xiè Lù 998 Hào Shǒu Yún Yī Yuàn（Yóuzhèng Biānmǎ：337580). Liánxì Diànhuà：55579787. Diànzǐ Yóuxiāng：bdrkh@cylxqmbv.health.cn

Han Zhen Zuoqiu, Shou Yun Hospital, 998 Tao Xie Road, Shunyi District, Beijing, China. Postal Code: 337580. Phone Number：55579787. E-mail：bdrkh@cylxqmbv.health.cn

120。姓名: 滑威盛

住址（机场）：中国北京市西城区钢刚路 781 号北京兵陆国际机场（邮政编码：844670）。联系电话：54494839。电子邮箱：wzhpj@rmzqhgca.airports.cn

Zhù zhǐ: Huá Wēi Chéng Zhōng Guó Běijīng Shì Xī Chéng Qū Gāng Gāng Lù 781 Hào Běijīng Bīng Liù Guó Jì Jī Chǎng（Yóuzhèng Biānmǎ：844670). Liánxì Diànhuà：54494839. Diànzǐ Yóuxiāng：wzhpj@rmzqhgca.airports.cn

Wei Cheng Hua, Beijing Bing Liu International Airport, 781 Gang Gang Road, Xicheng District, Beijing, China. Postal Code: 844670. Phone Number：54494839. E-mail：wzhpj@rmzqhgca.airports.cn

CHAPTER 5: NAME, SURNAME & ADDRESSES (121-150)

121。姓名: 全愈超

住址（博物院）：中国北京市西城区迅石路 642 号北京博物馆（邮政编码：461974）。联系电话：15479038。电子邮箱：cyjbi@rajhplft.museums.cn

Zhù zhǐ: Quán Yù Chāo Zhōng Guó Běijīng Shì Xī Chéng Qū Xùn Shí Lù 642 Hào Běijīng Bó Wù Guǎn (Yóuzhèng Biānmǎ: 461974). Liánxì Diànhuà: 15479038. Diànzǐ Yóuxiāng: cyjbi@rajhplft.museums.cn

Yu Chao Quan, Beijing Museum, 642 Xun Shi Road, Xicheng District, Beijing, China. Postal Code: 461974. Phone Number: 15479038. E-mail: cyjbi@rajhplft.museums.cn

122。姓名: 邹己进

住址（公司）：中国北京市昌平区歧德路 706 号国顺有限公司（邮政编码：878630）。联系电话：92620475。电子邮箱：wdslu@umjksofr.biz.cn

Zhù zhǐ: Zōu Jǐ Jìn Zhōng Guó Běijīng Shì Chāngpíng Qū Qí Dé Lù 706 Hào Guó Shùn Yǒuxiàn Gōngsī (Yóuzhèng Biānmǎ: 878630). Liánxì Diànhuà: 92620475. Diànzǐ Yóuxiāng: wdslu@umjksofr.biz.cn

Ji Jin Zou, Guo Shun Corporation, 706 Qi De Road, Changping District, Beijing, China. Postal Code: 878630. Phone Number: 92620475. E-mail: wdslu@umjksofr.biz.cn

123。姓名: 伊沛白

住址（医院）：中国北京市房山区仓坤路 651 号刚石医院（邮政编码：693839）。联系电话：66991700。电子邮箱：gldqt@giacsedq.health.cn

Zhù zhǐ: Yī Pèi Bái Zhōng Guó Běijīng Shì Fáng Shān Qū Cāng Kūn Lù 651 Hào Gāng Dàn Yī Yuàn (Yóuzhèng Biānmǎ: 693839). Liánxì Diànhuà: 66991700. Diànzǐ Yóuxiāng: gldqt@giacsedq.health.cn

Pei Bai Yi, Gang Dan Hospital, 651 Cang Kun Road, Fangshan District, Beijing, China. Postal Code: 693839. Phone Number：66991700. E-mail：gldqt@giacsedq.health.cn

124。姓名: 毛科亭

住址（寺庙）：中国北京市海淀区咚金路 277 号懂成寺（邮政编码：865292）。联系电话：41350809。电子邮箱：jintm@glyxiruc.god.cn

Zhù zhǐ: Máo Kē Tíng Zhōng Guó Běijīng Shì Hǎidiàn Qū Dōng Jīn Lù 277 Hào Dǒng Chéng Sì（Yóuzhèng Biānmǎ：865292）. Liánxì Diànhuà：41350809. Diànzǐ Yóuxiāng：jintm@glyxiruc.god.cn

Ke Ting Mao, Dong Cheng Temple, 277 Dong Jin Road, Haidian District, Beijing, China. Postal Code: 865292. Phone Number：41350809. E-mail：jintm@glyxiruc.god.cn

125。姓名: 终国源

住址（火车站）：中国北京市门头沟区锤翼路 348 号北京站（邮政编码：754666）。联系电话：61487460。电子邮箱：raozs@tjywcuzv.chr.cn

Zhù zhǐ: Zhōng Guó Yuán Zhōng Guó Běijīng Shì Méntóugōu Qū Chuí Yì Lù 348 Hào Běijīng Zhàn（Yóuzhèng Biānmǎ：754666）. Liánxì Diànhuà：61487460. Diànzǐ Yóuxiāng：raozs@tjywcuzv.chr.cn

Guo Yuan Zhong, Beijing Railway Station, 348 Chui Yi Road, Mentougou District, Beijing, China. Postal Code: 754666. Phone Number：61487460. E-mail：raozs@tjywcuzv.chr.cn

126。姓名: 濮阳胜坤

住址（公司）：中国北京市顺义区红乐路 414 号腾翰有限公司（邮政编码：773874）。联系电话：95771881。电子邮箱：bthko@gztcybux.biz.cn

Zhù zhǐ: Púyáng Shēng Kūn Zhōng Guó Běijīng Shì Shùnyì Qū Hóng Lè Lù 414 Hào Téng Hàn Yǒuxiàn Gōngsī (Yóuzhèng Biānmǎ：773874). Liánxì Diànhuà：95771881. Diànzǐ Yóuxiāng：bthko@gztcybux.biz.cn

Sheng Kun Puyang, Teng Han Corporation, 414 Hong Le Road, Shunyi District, Beijing, China. Postal Code: 773874. Phone Number：95771881. E-mail：bthko@gztcybux.biz.cn

127。姓名: 邱克星

住址（医院）：中国北京市朝阳区臻兵路 883 号食斌医院（邮政编码：739760）。联系电话：67419619。电子邮箱：idqtw@ldhjpoar.health.cn

Zhù zhǐ: Qiū Kè Xīng Zhōng Guó Běijīng Shì Zhāoyáng Qū Zhēn Bīng Lù 883 Hào Yì Bīn Yī Yuàn (Yóuzhèng Biānmǎ：739760). Liánxì Diànhuà：67419619. Diànzǐ Yóuxiāng：idqtw@ldhjpoar.health.cn

Ke Xing Qiu, Yi Bin Hospital, 883 Zhen Bing Road, Chaoyang District, Beijing, China. Postal Code: 739760. Phone Number：67419619. E-mail：idqtw@ldhjpoar.health.cn

128。姓名: 竺茂山

住址（机场）：中国北京市海淀区骥甫路 854 号北京友勇国际机场（邮政编码：142973）。联系电话：20263576。电子邮箱：kwpoc@ynzhtwla.airports.cn

Zhù zhǐ: Zhú Mào Shān Zhōng Guó Běijīng Shì Hǎidiàn Qū Jì Fǔ Lù 854 Hào Běijīng Yǒu Yǒng Guó Jì Jī Chǎng (Yóuzhèng Biānmǎ：142973). Liánxì Diànhuà：20263576. Diànzǐ Yóuxiāng：kwpoc@ynzhtwla.airports.cn

Mao Shan Zhu, Beijing You Yong International Airport, 854 Ji Fu Road, Haidian District, Beijing, China. Postal Code: 142973. Phone Number：20263576. E-mail：kwpoc@ynzhtwla.airports.cn

129。姓名: 牧敬毅

住址（广场）：中国北京市怀柔区禹易路 876 号毅晗广场（邮政编码：259198）。联系电话：20259999。电子邮箱：ymhiw@qbpgulxe.squares.cn

Zhù zhǐ: Mù Jìng Yì Zhōng Guó Běijīng Shì Huáiróu Qū Yǔ Yì Lù 876 Hào Yì Hán Guǎng Chǎng（Yóuzhèng Biānmǎ：259198). Liánxì Diànhuà：20259999. Diànzǐ Yóuxiāng：ymhiw@qbpgulxe.squares.cn

Jing Yi Mu, Yi Han Square, 876 Yu Yi Road, Huairou District, Beijing, China. Postal Code: 259198. Phone Number：20259999. E-mail：ymhiw@qbpgulxe.squares.cn

130。姓名: 熊茂迅

住址（湖泊）：中国北京市密云区陆波路 793 号盛禹湖（邮政编码：586092）。联系电话：24640941。电子邮箱：vbaxd@wvaejors.lakes.cn

Zhù zhǐ: Xióng Mào Xùn Zhōng Guó Běijīng Shì Mìyún Qū Lù Bō Lù 793 Hào Chéng Yǔ Hú（Yóuzhèng Biānmǎ：586092). Liánxì Diànhuà：24640941. Diànzǐ Yóuxiāng：vbaxd@wvaejors.lakes.cn

Mao Xun Xiong, Cheng Yu Lake, 793 Lu Bo Road, Miyun District, Beijing, China. Postal Code: 586092. Phone Number：24640941. E-mail：vbaxd@wvaejors.lakes.cn

131。姓名: 饶易亚

住址（公共汽车站）：中国北京市通州区守轼路 877 号维可站（邮政编码：633834）。联系电话：65593737。电子邮箱：apxmb@mzygvipq.transport.cn

Zhù zhǐ: Ráo Yì Yà Zhōng Guó Běijīng Shì Tōngzhōu Qū Shǒu Shì Lù 877 Hào Wéi Kě Zhàn（Yóuzhèng Biānmǎ：633834). Liánxì Diànhuà：65593737. Diànzǐ Yóuxiāng：apxmb@mzygvipq.transport.cn

Yi Ya Rao, Wei Ke Bus Station, 877 Shou Shi Road, Tongzhou District, Beijing, China. Postal Code: 633834. Phone Number：65593737. E-mail：apxmb@mzygvipq.transport.cn

132。姓名：廉晖骥

住址（寺庙）：中国北京市朝阳区近锤路 794 号冕星寺（邮政编码：763793）。联系电话：16087494。电子邮箱：higad@gjadtebz.god.cn

Zhù zhǐ: Lián Huī Jì Zhōng Guó Běijīng Shì Zhāoyáng Qū Jìn Chuí Lù 794 Hào Miǎn Xīng Sì（Yóuzhèng Biānmǎ：763793). Liánxì Diànhuà：16087494. Diànzǐ Yóuxiāng：higad@gjadtebz.god.cn

Hui Ji Lian, Mian Xing Temple, 794 Jin Chui Road, Chaoyang District, Beijing, China. Postal Code: 763793. Phone Number：16087494. E-mail：higad@gjadtebz.god.cn

133。姓名：向跃敬

住址（机场）：中国北京市怀柔区宝豪路 972 号北京毅帆国际机场（邮政编码：979104）。联系电话：62230033。电子邮箱：powsy@tgxmvysc.airports.cn

Zhù zhǐ: Xiàng Yuè Jìng Zhōng Guó Běijīng Shì Huáiróu Qū Bǎo Háo Lù 972 Hào Běijīng Yì Fān Guó Jì Jī Chǎng（Yóuzhèng Biānmǎ：979104). Liánxì Diànhuà：62230033. Diànzǐ Yóuxiāng：powsy@tgxmvysc.airports.cn

Yue Jing Xiang, Beijing Yi Fan International Airport, 972 Bao Hao Road, Huairou District, Beijing, China. Postal Code: 979104. Phone Number：62230033. E-mail：powsy@tgxmvysc.airports.cn

134。姓名：乜兵游

住址（寺庙）：中国北京市海淀区彬亮路 668 号际胜寺（邮政编码：793120）。联系电话：17956566。电子邮箱：hnvwk@dnwicgpz.god.cn

Zhù zhǐ: Niè Bīng Yóu Zhōng Guó Běijīng Shì Hǎidiàn Qū Bīn Liàng Lù 668 Hào Jì Shēng Sì（Yóuzhèng Biānmǎ：793120). Liánxì Diànhuà：17956566. Diànzǐ Yóuxiāng：hnvwk@dnwicgpz.god.cn

Bing You Nie, Ji Sheng Temple, 668 Bin Liang Road, Haidian District, Beijing, China. Postal Code: 793120. Phone Number：17956566. E-mail: hnvwk@dnwicgpz.god.cn

135。姓名: 微来强

住址（酒店）：中国北京市延庆区寰白路 844 号盛维酒店（邮政编码：332167）。联系电话：85933914。电子邮箱：wydiu@zvgudjpx.biz.cn

Zhù zhǐ: Wēi Lái Qiǎng Zhōng Guó Běijīng Shì Yánqìng Qū Huán Bái Lù 844 Hào Shèng Wéi Jiǔ Diàn（Yóuzhèng Biānmǎ：332167）. Liánxì Diànhuà：85933914. Diànzǐ Yóuxiāng：wydiu@zvgudjpx.biz.cn

Lai Qiang Wei, Sheng Wei Hotel, 844 Huan Bai Road, Yanqing District, Beijing, China. Postal Code: 332167. Phone Number：85933914. E-mail: wydiu@zvgudjpx.biz.cn

136。姓名: 邴彬自

住址（酒店）：中国北京市朝阳区坡不路 565 号亮钊酒店（邮政编码：949048）。联系电话：63989012。电子邮箱：cpxsi@pamcwvbo.biz.cn

Zhù zhǐ: Bǐng Bīn Zì Zhōng Guó Běijīng Shì Zhāoyáng Qū Pō Bù Lù 565 Hào Liàng Zhāo Jiǔ Diàn（Yóuzhèng Biānmǎ：949048）. Liánxì Diànhuà：63989012. Diànzǐ Yóuxiāng：cpxsi@pamcwvbo.biz.cn

Bin Zi Bing, Liang Zhao Hotel, 565 Po Bu Road, Chaoyang District, Beijing, China. Postal Code: 949048. Phone Number：63989012. E-mail: cpxsi@pamcwvbo.biz.cn

137。姓名: 季翼臻

住址（公园）：中国北京市石景山区自盛路 287 号铁淹公园（邮政编码：566762）。联系电话：38111284。电子邮箱：lkopb@gldaftzp.parks.cn

Zhù zhǐ: Jì Yì Zhēn Zhōng Guó Běijīng Shì Shíjǐngshān Qū Zì Shèng Lù 287 Hào Fū Yān Gōng Yuán（Yóuzhèng Biānmǎ：566762）. Liánxì Diànhuà：38111284. Diànzǐ Yóuxiāng：lkopb@gldaftzp.parks.cn

Yi Zhen Ji, Fu Yan Park, 287 Zi Sheng Road, Shijingshan District, Beijing, China. Postal Code: 566762. Phone Number：38111284. E-mail：lkopb@gldaftzp.parks.cn

138。姓名: 鞠澜继

住址（医院）：中国北京市通州区岐亮路 994 号钢盛医院（邮政编码：549541）。联系电话：56998061。电子邮箱：wnbeq@xdehyfus.health.cn

Zhù zhǐ: Jū Lán Jì Zhōng Guó Běijīng Shì Tōngzhōu Qū Qí Liàng Lù 994 Hào Gāng Shèng Yī Yuàn（Yóuzhèng Biānmǎ：549541）. Liánxì Diànhuà：56998061. Diànzǐ Yóuxiāng：wnbeq@xdehyfus.health.cn

Lan Ji Ju, Gang Sheng Hospital, 994 Qi Liang Road, Tongzhou District, Beijing, China. Postal Code: 549541. Phone Number：56998061. E-mail：wnbeq@xdehyfus.health.cn

139。姓名: 扶计伦

住址（公共汽车站）：中国北京市通州区稼智路 302 号坤桥站（邮政编码：823559）。联系电话：34147174。电子邮箱：jeytk@owrxeuym.transport.cn

Zhù zhǐ: Fú Jì Lún Zhōng Guó Běijīng Shì Tōngzhōu Qū Jià Zhì Lù 302 Hào Kūn Qiáo Zhàn（Yóuzhèng Biānmǎ：823559）. Liánxì Diànhuà：34147174. Diànzǐ Yóuxiāng：jeytk@owrxeuym.transport.cn

Ji Lun Fu, Kun Qiao Bus Station, 302 Jia Zhi Road, Tongzhou District, Beijing, China. Postal Code: 823559. Phone Number：34147174. E-mail：jeytk@owrxeuym.transport.cn

140。姓名: 胥自居

住址（公园）：中国北京市通州区振焯路 506 号大桥公园（邮政编码：395624）。联系电话：94658136。电子邮箱：dthkg@easkbzmn.parks.cn

Zhù zhǐ: Xū Zì Jū Zhōng Guó Běijīng Shì Tōngzhōu Qū Zhèn Chāo Lù 506 Hào Dà Qiáo Gōng Yuán (Yóuzhèng Biānmǎ：395624). Liánxì Diànhuà：94658136. Diànzǐ Yóuxiāng：dthkg@easkbzmn.parks.cn

Zi Ju Xu, Da Qiao Park, 506 Zhen Chao Road, Tongzhou District, Beijing, China. Postal Code: 395624. Phone Number：94658136. E-mail：dthkg@easkbzmn.parks.cn

141。姓名: 韩陆可

住址（火车站）：中国北京市房山区绅陆路 894 号北京站（邮政编码：830334）。联系电话：87074559。电子邮箱：lnvou@pnthckue.chr.cn

Zhù zhǐ: Hán Liù Kě Zhōng Guó Běijīng Shì Fáng Shān Qū Shēn Lù Lù 894 Hào Běijīng Zhàn (Yóuzhèng Biānmǎ：830334). Liánxì Diànhuà：87074559. Diànzǐ Yóuxiāng：lnvou@pnthckue.chr.cn

Liu Ke Han, Beijing Railway Station, 894 Shen Lu Road, Fangshan District, Beijing, China. Postal Code: 830334. Phone Number：87074559. E-mail：lnvou@pnthckue.chr.cn

142。姓名: 家钦中

住址（公园）：中国北京市房山区汉寰路 753 号南珏公园（邮政编码：209318）。联系电话：80319194。电子邮箱：nkcbo@hkdselaw.parks.cn

Zhù zhǐ: Jiā Qīn Zhōng Zhōng Guó Běijīng Shì Fáng Shān Qū Hàn Huán Lù 753 Hào Nán Jué Gōng Yuán (Yóuzhèng Biānmǎ：209318). Liánxì Diànhuà：80319194. Diànzǐ Yóuxiāng：nkcbo@hkdselaw.parks.cn

Qin Zhong Jia, Nan Jue Park, 753 Han Huan Road, Fangshan District, Beijing, China. Postal Code: 209318. Phone Number：80319194. E-mail：nkcbo@hkdselaw.parks.cn

143。姓名: 亢臻圣

住址（机场）：中国北京市海淀区亭沛路 714 号北京桥人国际机场（邮政编码：535768）。联系电话：59342897。电子邮箱：pzmst@nrzphjuo.airports.cn

Zhù zhǐ: Kàng Zhēn Shèng Zhōng Guó Běijīng Shì Hǎidiàn Qū Tíng Pèi Lù 714 Hào Běijīng Qiáo Rén Guó Jì Jī Chǎng（Yóuzhèng Biānmǎ：535768）. Liánxì Diànhuà：59342897. Diànzǐ Yóuxiāng：pzmst@nrzphjuo.airports.cn

Zhen Sheng Kang, Beijing Qiao Ren International Airport, 714 Ting Pei Road, Haidian District, Beijing, China. Postal Code: 535768. Phone Number：59342897. E-mail：pzmst@nrzphjuo.airports.cn

144。姓名: 百领陆

住址（公园）：中国北京市石景山区腾大路 301 号智轶公园（邮政编码：761622）。联系电话：23270183。电子邮箱：karlh@uvtrjoki.parks.cn

Zhù zhǐ: Bǎi Lǐng Liù Zhōng Guó Běijīng Shì Shíjǐngshān Qū Téng Dài Lù 301 Hào Zhì Yì Gōng Yuán（Yóuzhèng Biānmǎ：761622）. Liánxì Diànhuà：23270183. Diànzǐ Yóuxiāng：karlh@uvtrjoki.parks.cn

Ling Liu Bai, Zhi Yi Park, 301 Teng Dai Road, Shijingshan District, Beijing, China. Postal Code: 761622. Phone Number：23270183. E-mail：karlh@uvtrjoki.parks.cn

145。姓名: 单于发其

住址（公共汽车站）：中国北京市延庆区陆绅路 129 号甫维站（邮政编码：956280）。联系电话：38487529。电子邮箱：aumie@rxtaplbo.transport.cn

Zhù zhǐ: Chányú Fā Qí Zhōng Guó Běijīng Shì Yánqìng Qū Lù Shēn Lù 129 Hào Fǔ Wéi Zhàn（Yóuzhèng Biānmǎ：956280）. Liánxì Diànhuà：38487529. Diànzǐ Yóuxiāng：aumie@rxtaplbo.transport.cn

Fa Qi Chanyu, Fu Wei Bus Station, 129 Lu Shen Road, Yanqing District, Beijing, China. Postal Code: 956280. Phone Number：38487529. E-mail：aumie@rxtaplbo.transport.cn

146。姓名: 娄仲居

住址（广场）：中国北京市海淀区超沛路 537 号原澜广场（邮政编码：780591）。联系电话：22281730。电子邮箱：jashg@ibrmszyj.squares.cn

Zhù zhǐ: Lóu Zhòng Jū Zhōng Guó Běijīng Shì Hǎidiàn Qū Chāo Bèi Lù 537 Hào Yuán Lán Guǎng Chǎng （Yóuzhèng Biānmǎ：780591). Liánxì Diànhuà：22281730. Diànzǐ Yóuxiāng：jashg@ibrmszyj.squares.cn

Zhong Ju Lou, Yuan Lan Square, 537 Chao Bei Road, Haidian District, Beijing, China. Postal Code: 780591. Phone Number：22281730. E-mail：jashg@ibrmszyj.squares.cn

147。姓名: 邢龙铁

住址（寺庙）：中国北京市大兴区坚亚路 502 号可辙寺（邮政编码：484088）。联系电话：82505321。电子邮箱：psnwy@wfgbxpve.god.cn

Zhù zhǐ: Xíng Lóng Fū Zhōng Guó Běijīng Shì Dàxīng Qū Jiān Yà Lù 502 Hào Kě Zhé Sì （Yóuzhèng Biānmǎ：484088). Liánxì Diànhuà：82505321. Diànzǐ Yóuxiāng：psnwy@wfgbxpve.god.cn

Long Fu Xing, Ke Zhe Temple, 502 Jian Ya Road, Daxing District, Beijing, China. Postal Code: 484088. Phone Number：82505321. E-mail：psnwy@wfgbxpve.god.cn

148。姓名: 骆跃淹

住址（湖泊）：中国北京市昌平区中大路 488 号冠宽湖（邮政编码：525447）。联系电话：68599160。电子邮箱：dsiet@njyuxmsf.lakes.cn

Zhù zhǐ: Luò Yuè Yān Zhōng Guó Běijīng Shì Chāngpíng Qū Zhōng Dài Lù 488 Hào Guàn Kuān Hú (Yóuzhèng Biānmǎ：525447). Liánxì Diànhuà：68599160. Diànzǐ Yóuxiāng：dsiet@njyuxmsf.lakes.cn

Yue Yan Luo, Guan Kuan Lake, 488 Zhong Dai Road, Changping District, Beijing, China. Postal Code: 525447. Phone Number：68599160. E-mail：dsiet@njyuxmsf.lakes.cn

149。姓名: 伯顺洵

住址（机场）：中国北京市房山区际可路 712 号北京陶嘉国际机场（邮政编码：622918）。联系电话：30946333。电子邮箱：qwgzb@qjtsfzvr.airports.cn

Zhù zhǐ: Bó Shùn Xún Zhōng Guó Běijīng Shì Fáng Shān Qū Jì Kě Lù 712 Hào Běijīng Táo Jiā Guó Jì Jī Chǎng (Yóuzhèng Biānmǎ：622918). Liánxì Diànhuà：30946333. Diànzǐ Yóuxiāng：qwgzb@qjtsfzvr.airports.cn

Shun Xun Bo, Beijing Tao Jia International Airport, 712 Ji Ke Road, Fangshan District, Beijing, China. Postal Code: 622918. Phone Number：30946333. E-mail：qwgzb@qjtsfzvr.airports.cn

150。姓名: 宰来沛

住址（公园）：中国北京市东城区迅可路 228 号石食公园（邮政编码：970922）。联系电话：92558986。电子邮箱：ugdac@skyvfztm.parks.cn

Zhù zhǐ: Zǎi Lái Bèi Zhōng Guó Běijīng Shì Dōng Chéng Qū Xùn Kě Lù 228 Hào Dàn Yì Gōng Yuán (Yóuzhèng Biānmǎ：970922). Liánxì Diànhuà：92558986. Diànzǐ Yóuxiāng：ugdac@skyvfztm.parks.cn

Lai Bei Zai, Dan Yi Park, 228 Xun Ke Road, Dongcheng Area, Beijing, China. Postal Code: 970922. Phone Number：92558986. E-mail：ugdac@skyvfztm.parks.cn

Milton Keynes UK
Ingram Content Group UK Ltd.
UKHW051235010424
440421UK00012B/706